WHY THE RHINO SCATTERS HIS S#!T

Expanding Your Fun, Fulfillment, and Impact at Work

By Michael-John Bristow
and
Nigel J.A. Bristow

To the Storytellers of Africa
for their inspiration and timeless wisdom.

And to Devon and Beverley
who always let us know when we are full of it.

CONTENTS

*"There is no passion to be found
in playing small, in settling for a
life that is less than the one you
are capable of living."*

—Nelson Mandela

Introduction: Prisoners of Our Minds   **1**

Chapter 1: Why Rhino Scatters His S#!T   **5**

Chapter 2: The Wisdom of Mongoose   **37**

Chapter 3: Chicken and Dove   **61**

Chapter 4: A School for the Animals   **99**

Chapter 5: The Bear Who Dared   **121**

Chapter 6: Why Zebras Drink with Baboons   **139**

Chapter 7: Where on Earth is Timbuktu?   **159**

Conclusion: A Closing Note from the Author   **172**

Appendix

  Career Assessment   **174**

  Getting Connected   **179**

  Learning More   **180**

  References and Additional Reading   **182**

ACKNOWLEDGEMENTS

This book embodies principles we have practiced and taught for decades. We are indebted to our clients and thousands of participants in our coaching and career development workshops. Their questions, personal experiences and insightful comments enriched our thinking on the topics explored in this book.

We are especially grateful to those who helped us with their generous gifts of feedback. Input from the following people helped fine-tune our message, and encouraged us to see the project through to completion:

Conor Patrick, Annette Beatty, Liz Dixon, Ashley Fields, and Steve Rutledge.

We would also like to thank those who worked with us years ago on the original manuscript for the book "Flying the Coop":

Kathy Andrews, Kathleen Basoco, Bredow Bell, Matt Bertman, Mark Bregenzer, Craig Bristow, Patrick Bristow, Wanda Burghart, John Dietz, Marlene Feigenbaum, Davilyn Ferrin, Evelyn Francis, Larry Green, Jonathan Hardy, Sallie Hightower, Carol Incremona, Joe Incremona, Nan Macleod, Dave Radcliffe, Barbara Rice, Gavin Robertson, Marcelino

Sanchez, Sarah Sandberg, Justin Sapp, Anne Marie Staker, Neil Staker, Kennedy Thorley, Fred Turner, George Waller and Kee Meng Yeo. Special thanks go to Jim Bell, Tessa Santiago and Julia Mast for their many valuable suggestions.

We owe a debt of gratitude to the story tellers of the Angoni, Ashanti, Batonka and Masai peoples who inspired us with their fables. In recognition of their contribution to four of the stories in this book, we will contribute $1 from the proceeds of every book sold to support the education of children in Southern Africa.

Our deepest gratitude also to our spouses, Devon and Beverley. Without their support and enthusiasm, this book would never have made it into print.

INTRODUCTION
PRISONERS OF OUR BRAINS

"Nothing is so corrupting as a great idea whose time has passed."

—John P. Grier

Over the years, research has consistently shown that fewer than one-third of employees are engaged in their work (and almost 20% are actively *dis*engaged). Where do you fall? Do you experience work as just another job, or does it significantly enhance the quality of your life? Work should do much more than keep debt collectors at bay. It should be a meaningful pursuit that utilizes our talents and enables us to make a real difference. It should energize us and make us feel good about our accomplishments.

For decades we have helped people from all walks of life take control of their jobs and make a real difference at work. Whether at the beginning of your career or well beyond midpoint; whether suffering from a severe case of occupational blues or very satisfied with work; whether your boss is an effective leader or an ineffective bureaucrat; whether you wear a blue collar, a white collar, or a gold collar; regardless of your situation, the ideas we share in this book will equip you to expand your impact and find real fulfillment at work.

Harry Houdini (1874-1926) was one of history's most successful magicians. He became most famous for his ability to escape from almost any form of restraint, including chains, handcuffs, straight jackets, nailed crates, and even federal prison cells. A story is told, however, about one of his rare failures. While touring England, Houdini devised the kind of publicity stunt for which he was celebrated. He challenged the British prison authorities to create a lock he could not pick. The best locksmith in England was commissioned and the lock duly installed in a thick, steel prison door.

On the appointed day Houdini was marched into the dark, cramped prison cell. The door slammed shut and he set about picking the lock. It proved more challenging than expected. After half an hour he was no closer than when he had started. Another two hours of intense concentration yielded no progress. Mentally exhausted, Houdini leaned against the prison door handle. To his astonishment, the handle turned and the door swung open. He was free.

In all the excitement the guards had forgotten to lock the door. The great Houdini had been trapped in the prison cell for hours, not because of an insurmountable barrier outside himself but because of a faulty assumption. He was snared by his mistaken belief that the lock was actually, well, locked.

Unexamined assumptions can lead to similar consequences in our own careers. We often struggle and fall short not because we lack talent or creativity, but because we have acquired erroneous beliefs and habits along the way. For example, some think, "If I ask a lot of questions, others will believe I'm dumb." They mistakenly assume IQ is inversely proportional to the number of questions one asks and consequently ask too few. As a result, after arriving in new organizations, they take longer than average to learn how to work effectively and have a real impact. Paradoxically, their efforts to look smart end up making them foolish.

Often when we feel thwarted or frustrated in our careers, our first inclination is to identify barriers that reside outside ourselves. Upon closer reflection, however, we often find—as did Houdini—that we ourselves have built the very mental cages which limit our potential and rob us of fulfillment. These cages are built of our own beliefs and assumptions. Escape is not achieved simply by more analysis or harder work. Nor do we find freedom by hopping from one organization to another. Rather, escape requires new thinking. Within each of us lies a reservoir of untapped energy and talent. The purpose of this book is to identify the mindsets that help us engage that untapped potential.

Why the Rhino Scatters His S#!T uses seven entertaining parables—and compelling research in neuroscience and psychology—to address important questions and issues regarding success in 21st century organizations. Use this book to capture your thoughts and create a tailored blueprint for the future. Answer the questions at the end of each chapter. Identify old habits that are holding you back. Highlight new mindsets that will enable you to reach greater heights. Determine the actions you need to take. After finishing the book, follow through on your commitments, and experience the pleasure and power that come from taking control of your career and making a greater difference at work.

"Unlike other forms of life, man's greatest exertions are made in the pursuit not of necessities but of superfluities."

—Eric Hoffer

CHAPTER 1
WHY THE RHINO SCATTERS HIS S#!T

"Luck fights on the side of the prudent."

—Euripides

The classroom on the third floor was ordinary, bright—two dozen metal-framed desks, a lone podium, and a well-worn whiteboard. The room was filled with the banter of second-year executive MBA students. The class for which they had assembled had a reputation for being unusual. Consequently, their voices were driven by a current of anticipation and a hint of trepidation.

At five-thirty that evening, the door swung open and Professor Khumbulani marched in, placed his notes on the podium, and without even waiting for the students to sit, said, "Welcome to *Engage Yourself: Expanding Your Impact and Satisfaction at Work*. I teach this course via the interpretation of traditional African folktales. If you are wondering what African fables could possibly say about career management in modern organizations, let me assure you—you are not the first."

The students, who were still hanging jackets on the backs of chairs and getting settled, smiled.

Professor Khumbulani continued. "When these folktales were born," he said, "the term 'survival of the fittest' was not an abstract summary of evolutionary theory, but a daily reality. The intent of these stories, as they were passed from generation to generation, was to teach young members of the tribe how to survive—and hopefully thrive—in a hostile environment. Does that sound familiar?"

A few of the students nodded.

"If we were to describe the rules of a global economy, we would be hard-pressed to identify a more accurate term than "hostile environment." So, young tribesmen and tribeswomen, you must re-embrace survival of the fittest. These folktales will, you shall come to find, help you survive—and thrive—in today's hyper-competitive business environment.

"For most of our sessions," resumed the professor, "each of you will be in charge of your own learning. Your task over the next seven weeks is to discover for yourselves the specific principles that build and sustain a fun, fulfilling, and impactful career. If you can discover and clearly articulate these principles, you are on your way to an 'A' in this class—but, if you effectively *apply* these principles, your reward will be both greater fulfillment in your careers and, yes, financial peace of mind. Now, you are probably already aware that this is not your typical MBA class; do not expect me to hand you neatly packaged solutions to your career problems. Collectively, you already have the answers to most of your questions about career development. My task is to give you a process for tapping into those experiences and coming to your own conclusions. To that end, we are going to use a case study methodology, and, yes, most of these cases will be based on African folktales. At the beginning of each session, I will share a story—we will be getting to the first one momentarily—and you will discuss it in groups. Your task is to discover the principles within the parables, along with strategies for thriving in an environment where only the fittest survive.

"For all but two of the next seven weeks, you will work in self-selected groups of four or five. On the final day of class, I expect three things. First, each group is to submit a paper outlining its key lessons. It should be as long as is necessary to clearly make your points, and no longer. Second, each group will present a ten-minute summary of its conclusions to the class. Third, each of you will submit a personal career plan. The plan must map your goals four to five years out, and the concrete steps you are going to take over the next 12 months to move toward achieving those goals.

"With that in mind, our first folktale explores the male rhino's curious habit of scattering his dung with his hind legs. The Batonka people of southern Africa tell this story."

A very long time ago, before Zebra got her first stripe, a large and powerful female elephant held court near a popular waterhole on the African plains.

One day a young male rhino, newly free from his mother's watchful gaze, sauntered into the valley, hoping to find some territory he could call his own. All he wanted was a place thick with trees, an uncrowded watering hole, and, if at all possible, a wallow where he could spend lazy afternoons cooling himself in the rich, black mud.

Although his eyesight was among the weakest in the animal kingdom, his other senses were alert and awash with the sensations of his new surroundings. Winding his way through a thicket of leadwood trees, Rhino tasted the freshness of the air and smelled the cool, crisp water flowing nearby. In the distance, he heard Elephant trumpet commands with great bravado.

When Rhino emerged from the trees, he saw Elephant standing on a ridge above the waterhole. She looked down on the other animals. She alone decided where they were to drink and graze, and she dictated in what order they proceeded in their daily walk across the grassland. And behind her was the most perfect mud wallow Rhino had ever seen.

Rhino wanted that mud wallow. He wanted the stand of leadwood trees and the waterhole and the green grass that grew thick around it. He slipped in line between a zebra and a warthog who were on their way to the water and dreamed of running the valley himself.

It was hard to dream peacefully for long. Everywhere he went, Rhino could hear Elephant. She trumpeted her wishes across the valley. She flapped her ears fiercely, sending a crack of sound that shocked animals from their peaceful afternoon naps, and she often whomped her trunk on the ground to demand attention. Browbeaten, the animals always obeyed.

"Everyone else must be as tired of Elephant as I am," thought Rhino. "If I can replace her we will all be happier. Then the waterhole will be mine to run precisely as I choose."

By the end of the day Rhino had convinced himself that he was much smarter than Elephant. He knew— although he had not yet discussed this with anyone else—that the animals would rather he serve as leader.

"If I can prove I am better than Elephant, the others will rally around me," he thought. "She will have to give up her position as ruler of the waterhole."

Early the next morning, when the sun first stretched her delicate pink fingers across the horizon, Rhino walked up the ridge and, finding Elephant just blinking herself awake, challenged her to a duel; but it was not a duel of tusks, for Elephant would surely win, nor was it a duel of speed, nor cunning, for Rhino was outmatched in both of those as well. It was a duel, in fact, to see which of them could create the largest heap of dung.

Rhino knew this was the only arena in which he could emerge victorious. The animals gathered in silent anticipation and the duel commenced in the shade of the leadwood trees. In no time Rhino had produced a towering pile. It was, by all accounts, far larger than Elephant's, and from the ranks of the surprised spectators rose a cacophonous cheer.

This was Rhino's moment. He muscled his way to the edge of the ridge. "I am obviously more of a rhino than you'll ever be an elephant," he said. "We need a new leader here. It's time for you to move on."

Rhino swung his prodigious head in the direction of the crowd who, he thought, were thronging the banks in support of his coup. He expected to hear a roar of agreement to match their earlier cheer, but was met only with the droning of tsetse flies and the nervous cough of a teenage baboon. No one would meet his eye.

The animals knew of Elephant's temper. They knew her tusks would gore even the thick hide of an upstart rhino, and her feet would trample his head, prodigious or no. They knew.

Elephant knew, too.

She charged, all temper, tusks, bluster, and bellow. The thunder of hide crashing into hide sent birds from miles round into the great blue sky.

Gored, bleeding, bruised and broken, Rhino begged for mercy. Elephant had Rhino's head pinned to the ground with her large front foot. She cocked her head, fixing an amber eye on her hapless opponent.

"I'm so sorry," Rhino whimpered. "Please, let me go. I'll never challenge your rule again." But the admission was not to Elephant's satisfaction. She lowered a tusk to Rhino's quivering eyelid. "I promise, I promise I'll change my ways," said Rhino. "I'll leave this hole and find another. I'll never make another pile of dung as large as yours for as long as I live." Only then did Elephant remove her foot.

Rhino clambered up, caked in dust and blood, and limped away from the others and into the bush. He would never forget the lesson he learned at the waterhole. To this day, Rhino scatters his dung, just in case Elephant is watching.

"In a moment," said Professor Khumbulani, "you will form teams of four or five students and explore the connections between this parable and career management. Do not ask, 'What does the professor want us to find?' No single lesson is to be drawn. I want the discussions to build upon what your workplace experiences have already taught you. The lessons you find will be as diverse as those experiences. Have fun with it. You will learn a lot more by exploring your own insights than you will by trying to figure out what is in my head—which is not a pretty picture. The rest of the time is yours." Khumbulani picked up his papers and left the room.

"Is that it?" a student named Mike asked in disbelief. "A few minutes and an old fable? That's all we get for our tuition? What's *he* going to be doing?"

"Perhaps he finds more fulfillment on the golf course," joked Carlos, seated to Mike's left.

"His approach is different," said Denise, on Mike's right, "but that's why I signed up for the class. People who took this last semester said it was great. Someone in my strategy class called it the most useful course of his university career. I'm willing to give it a try."

Mike relented. "Maybe it's worth a shot. But you need to help me find the gem in this story or I'm going to find another class."

"If you three are going to be a team, may I join you?" asked Lily from the row behind.

Carlos, Lily, Denise, and Mike formed a circle. Denise began. "Perhaps it would be helpful to start by thinking of the main characters as organizational archetypes. Elephant is a CEO who runs the company like a feudal baron. Rhino is the ambitious newcomer who's chafing for change. And the rest of the animals are other members of the organization."

"That's a helpful way to frame this," agreed Lily. "And if you're Rhino—the new kid on the block—it's dangerous to let your mouth get ahead of your brain."

"That's exactly what happened here," said Carlos. "In high school I had a debate coach who would often tell us to 'think all that you speak, but don't speak all that you think.' Rhino's problem is he let his ego hijack his brain. I believe the basic message is that if we want to have successful careers, we mustn't let our egos draw us into battles with corporate elephants."

"Are you suggesting we just leave out-of-touch elephants to run the place anyway they please?" Mike asked. "Aren't we supposed to speak up when something is wrong? Just going along to get along doesn't sit well with me."

"I don't think it's a case of letting the old-guard do whatever they please, or about never challenging the status quo," said Denise. "It's good to challenge the status quo, but we should be more thoughtful about when and how we do it."

"I'll say one thing in Rhino's favor," said Mike. "He saw an obstacle and spoke directly to the person causing it. I know some chronic complainers who will gripe about a problem to everyone—except to the person creating the problem. If they really wanted to fix things they'd speak to the one responsible. But no, they talk to everybody else. It's gutless."

"So it's not a matter of *what* Rhino did. It's *how* he did it," said Lily.

"And why," added Carlos. "We should do what we do for the right reasons. All Rhino cared about was gaining control and being able to call the shots. He gave no thought to the other stakeholders and their needs. People like that invariably end up in trouble."

Lily leaned forward. "I agree. We usually give our support to those we trust to look out for the common good. Rhino's primary motivation was to elevate himself. It's no surprise the animals weren't willing to stick their necks out for him. Things would have gone a lot better for Rhino if he'd gotten to know the other animals first—if he'd found out what they were interested in and then tried to help them. But he was too impatient and self-absorbed to make that upfront investment."

"I agree," said Carlos. "I've seen this happen when new people are too eager to prove themselves. They have good intentions, so in that way they're not like Rhino, but they do share his impatience. They don't take the time to first understand the organization, how it works, and build a track record of meaningful accomplishments. Perhaps they're also a bit naïve; they think their textbook ideas will work anywhere. Either way, they get reckless and it hurts their credibility."

"That's a shame," said Denise, "because new employees often have the fresh ideas organizations need. Once again it's an issue of ego getting in the way. They don't want to stop and ask for direction."

"In my experience," said Lily, "some new people try too hard to look smart. They mistakenly think the fewer questions they ask the smarter they'll look. In reality, the smartest new hires are usually the ones who aren't afraid to ask questions."

"Agreed," said Carlos. "The first thing I tell new employees is to establish their technical credibility by doing quality work. Once they have the technical credibility, then they can worry about the organizational knowledge that will help them expand their impact."

"Rhino also made the mistake of surprising the animals around the waterhole," said Denise. "Surprise may be useful against your enemies, but it's a lousy way to get the support of potential allies."

"Exactly," said Mike. "In one of my other classes we've been learning about the politics of innovation. People who are good at selling their ideas don't use formal meetings and proposals to get buy-in. They use meetings and proposals to show the last of the resistors they already have the support of key players in the organization. One of Rhino's mistakes was he didn't take the time to build support before making his grand announcement. He ignored the politics of change."

Denise nodded. "You used the word politics. Some people think politics is automatically a bad thing when it's not. Politics is simply the art of persuasion. Without politics the status quo would last forever."

"I guess politics is one of those necessary evils," said Lily.

"Not in my view," said Mike. "Politics is a necessary *good*. The process of going to people one on one to get their support also involves getting their input. When I share my idea with potential backers, they will usually give me some feedback. I then take that feedback and adapt my plans to address their concerns, which makes my idea even better. That's politics."

"Don't you run the risk of losing control of your idea?" Carlos asked.

"I think it's a risk worth taking. Involving others does mean you have to give up some control, but you get a lot more in return. For one, their input almost always results in a better plan. Second, because their ideas become a part of the plan, they're more likely to feel some ownership and vocally support it."

"That's a view of politics I've never considered," admitted Lily.

Mike continued. "Rhino reminds me of people who, to paraphrase John F. Kennedy, only ask what the company can do for them rather than what they can do for the company. They're only interested in the next promotion, not what is best for all stakeholders."

Lily said, "The rhinos I know are also more focused on making a dollar than on having a greater impact. In our strategy and business policy class we looked at research about the relationship between company mission statements and profitability. It turns out that companies with profit-focused mission statements are, on average, less profitable than companies with customer-focused mission statements. Maybe the same is true for individuals. Being too preoccupied with short-term financial interests can be self-defeating."

"I think you're right," said Mike. "People who focus on promotions rather than on making a difference often come up short in both areas."

"Another problem with focusing on promotions is that companies keep restructuring," said Denise. "I've realized that as my company continues to flatten, fewer people get steady promotions. A coworker once told me that because he was no longer being promoted regularly, he no longer had a career. That's like saying most school teachers and medical doctors don't have careers, which is absurd."

"It's interesting you mention that," Mike said. "I recently took a career development workshop at our company. We were encouraged to define 'career' as a path of increasing ability and contribution, rather than just a ladder leading to higher and higher positions. What do you think?"

"I like it. Defining careers in terms of promotions limits my ability to control my own future. I don't control which positions in the organization will open up, or who will select the person to fill that vacancy. So thinking about my career too much in terms of promotions puts the control of my career in the hands of those who control the promotions. That's why it makes sense for me to think of my career in terms of increasing ability and contribution. Those are things I have a lot more influence over. So as long as I think of my career in those terms, I'm in the driver's seat.

Also, since our organization structure was recently flattened—for the fifth time—there are even fewer rungs on the ladder to aspire to."

"In my company," said Carlos, "they haven't just removed the rungs from the career ladder. They've greased the uprights! But seriously, this makes a lot of sense. It does seem more empowering to frame career growth in terms of increasing ability and contribution, but that's not how I've generally thought of it. In fact, separating promotions from career growth sounds almost countercultural. I'm going to have to give that some more thought."

"Can we go back to the issue of speaking up and disagreeing with others?" asked Lily. "My concern is that we've been talking about the politics of building support and picking our battles carefully, but our discussion seems to be based on the assumption that disagreeing with others will always provoke a backlash. Are we making that assumption?"

"Possibly," said Mike, "but not without some justification. If you want to be influential in an organization, you've got to be willing to speak up. Speaking up always entails some risk, especially when it's an important issue that everyone is running from. If everyone's avoiding it, it's probably because they're scared of offending someone important."

"That's true," said Carlos. "And if you offend one of the corporate elephants, you'd better be ready to deal with the repercussions."

"I don't think we should give so much weight to the issue of offending corporate elephants," said

Lily. "Most of our day-to-day disagreements involve colleagues, not company bigwigs. And even when a disagreement is with an executive, it's not going to automatically provoke a backlash."

"I think Lily's onto something," said Denise. "We may be creating a false dichotomy if we say our only choices are, 'Speak up and provoke a backlash,' or, 'Keep quiet and preserve the relationship.' You lose something either way. I think if you're skilled at it you can speak up and preserve the relationship at the same time."

"You might be able to pull that off with some people, but not everyone," said Mike.

"That doesn't mean we shouldn't try."

"So how do you disagree with or challenge someone without provoking a negative reaction?"

"I don't have all the answers, but I do think most of us could benefit from learning to disagree more agreeably. When I studied behavioral psychology I learned that small changes to the words we use often lead to significant differences in how others respond. Disagreeing agreeably is about stating your disagreement in a way that doesn't put others on the defensive. It's about building on the ideas of others rather than picking them apart."

"How do you do that?" asked Carlos.

"For one," said Denise, "I try to do some things I learned in a coaching skills class. Whenever I can, I use questions to help others think through the issue for themselves. People don't always buy *my* conclusions, but they love to buy their own. Thought-provoking questions often create more clarity than well-reasoned arguments."

"Can you give me an example?" said Carlos.

"Sure. If someone has a proposal and it appears they've overlooked the needs of stakeholders, I don't say, 'You've ignored your stakeholders. This plan will never fly.' As true as that statement may be, it will likely prompt them to try and prove me wrong, or to exclude me from the rest of the conversation. Instead I might ask questions like, 'Who are your stakeholders? What are each of their interests, and what will they be looking for in the proposal?' That way they discover the holes in their proposal for themselves."

Carlos nodded. "That makes a lot of sense. Instead of pushing your solutions onto them, they come up with their own answers, which builds ownership."

"Exactly. I also try to avoid certain words that trigger defensiveness," said Denise. "Words like 'you're wrong,' 'I disagree' and 'yes, but.'"

"Wait, what's so bad about the word 'but'?" asked Carlos. "Most of us use that word dozens of times a day. All of us have done it in this conversation alone."

"Let me give an example. Say someone on my team makes a bold, creative suggestion, and I agree with 80 percent of it. If that's the case, I should start with what I like about the suggestion. I think most people begin with some form of agreement, then almost immediately they deny the agreement by inserting the word 'but.' They might say, 'I really like the idea, but marketing won't buy it.' The moment they say 'but,' they verbally erase the notion they liked the idea. In the other person's mind, the brief statement of agreement is simply a manipulative ploy. It was thrown in only to soften the blow of disagreement. The only thing the other person believes is what comes after the 'but.'"

"I can see that. However, you can't just ignore things you disagree with. You've got to speak up about your concerns."

"Nice try," said Denise with a smile. "Substituting the word 'however' for 'but' means pretty much the same thing."

Carlos paused, then threw up his hands. "You got me. So how do you talk about your concerns without using words like 'but' or 'however?'"

"I try to build on the part of the idea I appreciate. So instead of saying, 'I really like your idea, but marketing won't buy it,' I say, 'I really like your idea. It's bold and creative. As you know, marketing will have to sign off on it. What thoughts do you have for getting marketing on board?' Now instead of feeling slammed by the words 'but marketing won't buy it,' the other person feels encouraged to share more of their thinking."

"That definitely feels more respectful. What about the other words you mentioned, like telling someone they're wrong?"

"Most people are far too quick to use that word," Denise said. "Telling people they're wrong just gets their defenses up. So if someone says, 'To fix this you've got to do A and B,' and I know they've missed step C, I don't say, 'That's wrong, you forgot about step C.' Instead I say, 'That's right, and in addition to what you said about A and B, be sure to finish it up with C.'"

"That makes sense. You also said you avoid the words, 'I disagree.' If you really do disagree, aren't you supposed to be honest and say so?"

"I'm not saying we should never use the word 'disagree.' It's just not usually necessary. Let's go back to the example I used a moment ago. If they left out step C, don't say, 'I disagree. You left out step C.' Instead say, 'I agree, steps A and B are essential. It's also important to wrap up the process with step C.' If I already agree with two-thirds of their plan, why start with the points where I disagree?"

"I like how you framed that, because you're not just being more tactful. You're also being more accurate, which makes it easier for the other person to accept the feedback."

"Not only are you being more accurate; you're starting with your areas of agreement rather than areas of disagreement. By focusing on areas of agreement first, we encourage openness on both sides," said Lily.

"This sounds like we're supposed to be lawyers, measuring every word before we speak it," said Mike. "We work with adults. We shouldn't have to walk on eggshells all the time. If I disagree with something, I should say so, and I should do it directly so there's no misunderstanding. If people disagree with me, they're welcome to speak plainly in return. The professor said this is about survival of the fittest. Open debate is the only way to ensure the best ideas survive."

"You make a valid point," said Denise. "When you achieve a climate of complete openness and disclosure, direct debate works great. So tell me, Mike, when you have disagreements in your organization, do some people tend to back down quicker than others?"

"Obviously."

"And why do they back down?"

"Because their ideas can't take the scrutiny."

"That could be true. Let's say their ideas *can* take the scrutiny. What else might cause them to retreat?"

"A lack of confidence," admitted Mike.

"A conflict-avoidant personality," said Lily.

"Those reasons also make a lot of sense. Anything else?" asked Denise.

"They might be worried about offending someone," added Carlos, "like the animals at the waterhole. They wouldn't do anything that might provoke Elephant."

"And some people just want to avoid any chance of causing offense, even when they know the other person wouldn't—or couldn't—retaliate," said Lily.

"That's right," said Denise. "When people automatically defer to others because they don't want to cause offense, or they lack confidence or status, or they don't like conflict, or they feel intimidated, then the best ideas never come out. If you really want the best ideas, you need to get everyone fully participating, including your most reserved players."

"I agree with Denise," said Lily. "People don't open up unless they feel safe. Disagreeing without being disagreeable will help with that. When we challenge others too forcefully, we often silence them. We then deceive ourselves into thinking we won, but it's a far cry from actually getting them over to our side."

"That's right," said Carlos. "Unless you win the other person's *support*, you haven't won the argument in any way that really matters. In my experience, expressing strong disagreement seldom converts the opposition. It either shuts them up or it strengthens their determination to defend their ideas at any cost."

"There's research to support that," said Denise. "It's called the backfire effect. Scientists at Dartmouth found that when someone has a deep, established belief—like a religious or political belief—presenting that person with contradictory evidence can actually make their beliefs *stronger*. That's why arguing with strangers on the internet is often a pointless endeavor; people just become more entrenched in their original beliefs."

"Okay, you've won me over," Mike said. "At first I thought your ideas for disagreeing agreeably were too warm and fuzzy, but they aren't. They even worked on me. I have to admit, questions can be more powerful than arguments."

"If I understand this correctly," said Carlos, "disagreeing agreeably begins with finding something you can agree with and building from there. What if you can't find anything to agree with?"

"Then you're probably not looking hard enough," suggested Lily. "There's almost always going to be something you can agree on."

"I assume that everyone I work with is reasonably intelligent," said Denise. "So if I disagree with 90 percent of someone's plan, it's probably because I don't really understand where they're coming from. Instead of jumping in and unloading all my misgivings, I force myself to ask them a few questions."

"Like what?" asked Mike.

"I usually ask four basic things. First, 'What do you want to achieve with this? What outcomes are you looking for?' Second, 'What options have you considered?' Third, 'What criteria did you use to identify the best option?' And fourth, 'What do you see as the pros and cons of your preferred option as opposed to the other options?' When I ask people open-ended questions like these, and really try to listen to their answers with an open mind, I come out of the discussion with a lot more room for agreement. If they've missed something important, the questions help them figure it out without me forcing my opinions on them. I also find that by asking questions I often discover their idea was solid to begin with."

Denise continued. "Our brains are wired to focus on the negative. It's called negativity bias; we find it innately easier to focus on what's wrong with what someone is saying. But I've found my initial misgivings are usually because I don't understand their idea, not because it was wrong."

"What if that doesn't happen?" asked Mike. "What if you do all that and you still believe they're wrong?"

"I'll start by summarizing what they told me about their idea, then I'll ask if I've portrayed it fairly or if I've missed anything. The way I see it, before I can legitimately criticize someone else's thoughts, I've got to earn that right. I earn it by working to understand their idea as well as they do themselves."

"That makes sense. So what do you do after you've earned the right to criticize?"

"Once *they're* convinced I understand their idea, I change course and talk about my concerns. I might say something like, 'I think you and I are looking at this from two different angles. Do you mind if I describe things as I see them?' No one has ever told me no."

"That must take a lot of time."

Denise nodded. "It does seem that way at first glance. What I've experienced is usually the opposite. Because I've listened to the other person with respect and shown a genuine willingness to see things from their point of view, they're more inclined to return the favor by listening openly to my concerns. A lot of people think listening takes time. In my experience, *not* listening takes much more time."

"How so?"

"When I don't work to first understand the other person's point of view, I find I waste a lot of effort repeating myself, because the other person is still stuck on their standpoint and won't listen. Then they keep repeating themselves because they don't feel heard. The end result is we waste a lot of time going around in circles, throwing verbal punches but never connecting. I'm convinced the art of influence has more to do with listening than it does with talking. Good listeners are usually more influential than good talkers."

"Even though this is a great approach, it's not going to work every time," warned Mike. "I doubt Rhino could have won Elephant over to his way of thinking, no matter how tactful he was."

"You're right," said Denise. "That's why I keep my résumé up to date. Sometimes you're going to get a negative reaction no matter how skillful and diplomatic you are. If you want to have influence in an organization, being tactful is important, but it isn't enough. Sometimes you have to be willing to ruffle some feathers, and it's easier to take that risk when you know you have other waterholes you can migrate to."

"I'm glad you said that," replied Lily. "I think I can be too tactful. I sometimes find myself shying away from difficult but critical conversations."

"Speaking up has never been a problem for me," said Mike, "but being tactful is a different story. It just dawned on me that I've been focused on the wrong goal. I've always focused on winning arguments rather than winning support."

"I think you have a lot of company," said Denise. "We win the battle but lose the war. Leaders need to worry less about the people who openly disagree with them and more about those who hide disagreement. Bosses like Elephant either lose their best people or end up with a disengaged and hostile workforce."

"This discussion has been surprisingly helpful," said Mike. "I had my doubts, but this really could be a useful process. I'll stay for at least one more week."

Lily smiled. "Glad to hear it. Maybe the prof isn't as unhinged as you thought."

"I'd like to go back to one of Mike's earlier comments," said Carlos. "It may be the core issue in this story. Mike said Rhino reminded him of people who are too focused on what the company can do for them rather than on what they can do for the company. The more value you add, the more others are willing to let you influence them. Rhino didn't understand that and neither do a lot of managers at my company. They think their title gives them power, when in reality it doesn't. What gives them power is how they use their position to make great things happen—for their people as well as the company."

"Absolutely," said Denise. "There's a lot to be said for the informal power that comes from a track record of accomplishment."

"I agree with the importance of informal power," said Mike. "At the same time, there's a lot to be said for power that comes from one's position. Some elephants out there wield a lot of formal power even though they may not always add a lot of value. We ignore their power at our own peril."

Denise nodded. "I'd like to say you're wrong, but I agree we can't ignore formal power. By the way, what are Rhino's chances of making a comeback? In the story he slinked off into the bush and never again tried to change things. He didn't learn anything useful from his mistakes. He only learned to be permanently submissive to Elephant."

An animated discussion followed. Everyone knew people like Rhino—people who undermine themselves by putting others down, picking the wrong battles, and hogging the limelight. Lily and Mike also knew a few who were able to turn their careers around even after losing ill-conceived battles with corporate elephants.

At the end of their discussion the group identified five principles for building influence in an organization:

- **Don't try to make yourself look good at the expense of others. Control your ego.**
- **Don't surprise the people you rely on for support. Build informal support before trying to get formal approval.**
- **Build your informal power:**
  - **Focus on winning support rather than winning arguments.**
  - **Learn to disagree agreeably (e.g., avoid phrases such as "you're wrong," "I disagree," "yes, but," etc.).**
  - **Build on the ideas of others rather than dismissing them.**
  - **Rely on open-ended questions more than polished arguments.**
  - **Master the art of listening.**
  - **Maximize the value you add. Your power to influence is directly linked to the value you bring others.**
- **Pick your battles carefully. Make sure they address important issues and serve the common good.**
- **Retain control of your career by expanding your impact rather than focusing on getting the next promotion.**

THE DUNNING-KRUGER EFFECT:
AVOIDING THE RHINO TRAP

"Ignorance more frequently begets confidence than does knowledge."

—Charles Darwin

One sunny morning in 1995, a man named MacArthur Wheeler began a brand-new career: armed robbery. Thus it was that he marched into two banks in Pittsburg, Pennsylvania and demanded money at gunpoint. He did this in broad daylight, with no visible attempt to hide his face from cameras or from other people.

Police reviewed the security footage and arrested Wheeler the very same day. When detectives showed him the surveillance tapes, he looked shocked. "But I wore the juice," he insisted. It turned out Wheeler had covered his face in lemon juice under the mistaken belief that since lemon juice can be used to create invisible ink, it would also make his face invisible.

This is one of countless stories of humans doing wondrously stupid things. It was the inspiration for later research by David Dunning and Justin Kruger at Cornell University. They found that the less competent an individual, the more likely that individual was to overestimate their own skill. In the study, those on the low end of the competence scale rated their performance to be five times higher than it actually was. These subjects remained unable to recognize and acknowledge their own lack of skill even after receiving training that highlighted how much they still had to learn. Later research found that even though highly skilled individuals also tend to overestimate their own performance, their self-assessments are not as detached from reality.

Like Rhino, most of us have a tendency to overestimate our own skill level and to assume that others see us in the same rosy light. This is why reality shows like American Idol can be so entertaining. It's not the great performers who most pique our interest; it's the terrible performers who *think* they are great that make the show so captivating. Watching them, we can't help but wonder how they could possibly have thought they would be competitive.

The truth is we all suffer from equally large blind spots. Fortunately for us, they aren't broadcast on national TV. The Dunning-Kruger effect is a subset of what is called self-serving bias. We are inclined to see ourselves as above average in the majority of cases. When the authors of this book teach workshops, they use anonymous voting technology to poll participants. One of their favorite questions is, "How competent are you as a driver?" There are only two options: above average and below average. Now, mathematically speaking, it is impossible for more than half the population to be above average. If people saw themselves accurately, the responses should be close to a 50/50 split. It has never happened. After polling hundreds of classes and thousands of people, the split is 82/18. Out of thousands of participants, 82% think they are above-average drivers.

The vast majority of us believe we are better performers than we actually are in most walks of life. We think we are funnier and more attractive, that we work harder, that we are more polite, that we are more politically informed, etc. And if you say to yourself, "*I* don't think that way," you are claiming to be above average in regard to your own self-awareness. Trapped again!

Our bias towards optimism is why most of us think we can drive perfectly safely while speaking on our cell phones. We believe rules and warning signs were created not for ourselves, but for other, less gifted people. As with Rhino, this leads to over-confidence that can cause serious mistakes in our lives and careers. It also makes us not as likely to heed the warnings of others, because we implicitly assume we are more intelligent than those giving the advice.

Although these psychological effects appear entirely dysfunctional, your brain's self-delusion is not a bug; it's a feature. Research has found that those who have these positive delusions are happier than those with more realistic views of their skills. It is hypothesized that such a bias has an evolutionary advantage. Those who are happier—and think they can do more than their natural abilities would suggest—are more likely to take on new challenges, which means they tend to learn more and achieve more.

Research from Suzanne Sergerstrom confirms that those who are more positive are also more persistent when engaged in difficult tasks. They persevere despite initial mistakes and failures, whereas those who are too preoccupied with their shortcomings are more likely to avoid new challenges, or to give up at the first sign of difficulty, thereby depriving themselves of growth opportunities and important breakthroughs. Optimists are also less likely to become depressed or anxious, and they get ill less often.

So self-delusion is not entirely bad. The key to success is cultivating a sense of realistic optimism. Realistic optimism is achieved by balancing our confidence with honest feedback from others, reigning in our defensiveness when others tell us what they really think of our ideas, and adapting our plans based on the insights we gain from others. Candid feedback gives us critical information to counter the blind confidence that leads to spectacular failure. If Rhino had run his plans by a few friends first, he may have found a more effective way to achieve the change he was hoping for.

We are all awesome—just not as awesome as we'd like to think. Cultivating a sense of realistic optimism will grant us the mental-health benefits of rose-colored glasses without the dangerous distortions of a fun-house mirror.

"A large portion of our trouble is caused by too much bone in the head and not enough in the back."

—Unknown

APPLICATION EXERCISE

Given your insights from this folktale and the ideas that came out of the group discussion, what can you do to achieve greater influence and success at work? Be as specific as you can.

- **What beliefs or practices are preventing you from exercising greater influence in your organization? What battles are you fighting that do not serve the common good?**

  _____

  _____

  _____

  _____

  _____

  _____

  _____

- **What can you do to add more value for your colleagues? What can you do to help others do their work more effectively? What can you do to serve the common good?**

  _____

  _____

  _____

  _____

  _____

  _____

  _____

- What can you do to improve your ability to disagree agreeably? What can you do to win support rather than win arguments?

_____

_____

_____

_____

_____

_____

- What can you do to make sure your bias for optimism doesn't lead to your own downfall?

_____

_____

_____

_____

_____

_____

_____

"Often a dash of judgment is better than a flash of genius."

—Howard W. Newton

CHAPTER 2
THE WISDOM OF MONGOOSE

"Our doubts are traitors, and make us lose the good we oft might win by fearing to attempt."

—William Shakespeare,
Measure for Measure

"Good morning," said Professor Khumbulani, striding into the room and placing his papers on the lectern. The class quieted and took their seats. "I trust you found some pearls among the dung in Rhino's story. Today's folktale comes from the Masai people of Kenya. It introduces the topics of courage and planning, which are at the heart of career satisfaction. Before I share the story of the mongoose, the lion, and the ostrich—I must share a little about the domestic arrangements of ostriches. It is important to know that in ostrich society, the children are cared for primarily by the father.

In the warm light of the rising sun, the animals gathered on the riverbank to drink. Just beyond the river's bend, in a small stand of saltbush, tall Father Ostrich stood guard over his nest. The young father puffed his black chest feathers with pride, for in the nest slept eight spotted brown chicks, recently hatched.

Weeks before, he had scraped the sandy ground with his powerful feet, as he had seen his father do, and in the swale his wife had laid her eggs. Then he sat. He warmed the eggs through the long nights. He drove off jackals, vultures, and wild dogs who loved nothing more than a fresh ostrich egg in the morning. He ate sparingly, having little time between shifts to chase lizards or find grass seed close to his nest, and he drank even less than he ate.

Father Ostrich could hear the honks and snorts and whinnies of animals gathering for their morning drink. He watched his wife pick her way along the riverbank, head aswivel, searching for food, when an uncommonly strong thirst overcame him. Certain his fledglings would be safe for the few seconds necessary to gulp a drink, Father Ostrich hurried to the river. His long legs carried him swift and true. He regularly turned his head to check on the nest as he ran. Upon reaching the river he put his head down for the briefest of moments to indulge in the cool, crisp water. Alas, it was a moment too long. When he looked up, three chicks were missing.

He rushed back to the nest, but Mother Ostrich was already waiting. She had not taken long to notice the missing children, or her missing husband. Feathers flew—black and white and brown. But mostly black.

As a final feather floated to the ground, Mother Ostrich noticed a set of fresh tracks leading away from the nest: lion prints, followed by three sets of tiny ostrich prints. Mother Ostrich flew across the sand, through the grass and past the thorn trees, at a speed few on the savannah could match. She scanned the grassland for movement. Then, out of the corner of her eye and near a towering termite mound, she saw a most peculiar sight: Lion, half asleep, curled around three ostrich chicks.

"Lion," she demanded, "return my children."

Lion yawned languidly and extended his claws. "Nonsense," he said. "These are not your children. They are my cubs. See how they follow me? See how they snuggle close to keep warm?"

The two argued. Ostrich bobbed and weaved and flapped her mighty wings, but nothing could persuade Lion to release her children. Finally, Ostrich resolved to take up the issue with the Council of Elders, who spent their days keeping peace among animals in the valley. She turned from Lion and bolted, reaching the council while the sun was still high.

Ostrich presented her case most eloquently. Meerkat nodded in sympathy. Aardvark curled into a ball and wiped away tears with a long, pink tongue. The story silenced even Hyena, who could find nothing whatsoever to laugh about. The Council resolved to send a delegation to Lion.

The solemn procession wove its way to the anthill. The animals gasped in disbelief, and some snickered, to see the ostrich chicks nestled between Lion's paws.

Anybody in their right mind knew those were not Lion's cubs. Aardvark was just about to demand the return of the chicks when he noticed the sharpness of Lion's claws. Meerkat noticed the length of Lion's teeth. Hyena noticed the strength of Lion's haunches.

The council withdrew to a clump of red oat grass where, after speedy deliberation, they concluded the chicks were, in fact, Lion's cubs. They returned to the anthill to announce their verdict.

Ostrich was outraged. She beat the ground with her feet. She beat the air with her wings. She looked fit to tie her neck into knots. A general meeting of the animals was now her only option. Enlisting the help of her mournful husband and the pale chanting goshawk, she gathered the inhabitants of the valley.

After the animals had assembled, Ostrich pled her case. "Lion has stolen my three chicks," she accused, bobbing her head for dramatic effect. "He refuses to return them. He thinks, if you can believe this, they are his. Have you ever heard such a thing?" Her feathers ruffled in a wave of grief.

Silently, Lion uncurled his body from around the sleeping chicks. He carefully placed one lily pad-sized paw in front of the other and stretched his long, lithe, tawny body so his muscles rippled menacingly in the morning sun. He opened his mouth and yawned as unnerving a yawn as any creature had ever seen. One could have counted his molars, if one had a mind to. The animals had no such mind. Almost immediately they too concluded the chicks were Lion's cubs.

All, except Mongoose.

Mongoose was late to the meeting that day. But since the rear entrance to her underground den opened right near the base of the anthill, she made it just in time for the ruling. As the animals announced their absurd conclusion, Mongoose stuck her head out her back door. What she saw was patently absurd: a fully-grown lion acting like the proud father of what were clearly three baby ostrich chicks.

"What do you mean, 'These must be Lion's cubs'?" barked Mongoose. "Since when did lion cubs have feathers? It's obvious they belong to Ostrich!"

Lion was enraged. With a throaty roar and a flick of his black-tipped tail, he leaped at Mongoose, but he swatted at empty air and his teeth snapped shut on a shower of dust. Mongoose was already safe inside the tunnels of her den.

In all the fuss and dust and roars and snapping teeth, grateful Mother Ostrich gathered her chicks and hurried them away.

Lion was set on killing Mongoose. He laid siege to her home. Little did he know, a mongoose den never has only one entrance. So while Lion lay panting, day after day in the hot African sun, Mongoose was free to come and go through her many other entrances.

Professor Khumbulani smiled. "The rest of the time is yours," he said. Mike sighed, but joined his friends as the study groups assembled.

Carlos began. "This story reminds me of people at reputable companies who do things that lack integrity, like the animals on the committee. They were so scared of Lion that they were willing to condone a chicknapping. When people feel vulnerable, they're more likely to compromise their ethics."

"That certainly happens," said Lily, "but I don't think ethical or moral breakdowns are the major issue here. Most companies are pretty ethical, and most leaders want to do the right thing."

"I'm not sure I agree. Look at some of the huge financial scandals we see from time to time. The executives implicated in those scandals couldn't have cooked their company's books without the silence of dozens of people at lower levels. When potential whistle-blowers feel vulnerable, they'd rather choke on their whistles than blow them, and when that happens it doesn't take long for an organization to go from being a bureaucracy to a kleptocracy."

"Okay—a bit harsh—but, yes, I agree," said Lily. "If people at lower levels always had the courage to speak up, we'd have fewer ethical meltdowns to contend with. Even so, these scandals involve a relatively small number of corporations, which is why I see the implications of this story a little differently."

"Fair enough. What are the implications to you?"

"Well, for me, it's more about how being vulnerable discourages us from expressing our views openly. I admit sometimes I won't challenge my boss on simple day-to-day operating decisions, even though my pushback could make the team more effective. My lack of openness won't be on the evening news, and in most cases the cost to the organization will be minimal. But multiply that cost by millions of employees keeping their opinions to themselves and it adds up fast. I think every company would benefit if their employees were a little braver, like Mongoose."

"I'm not sure bravery was the key issue," Denise said. "Rhino was brave, too, and look where it got him. It isn't that Mongoose was braver than the other animals. What the others lacked, that she had, was a safety net. Mongoose knew Lion could swallow her whole, but she also knew he would have to catch her first. Having the security of other entrances gave her the confidence to challenge Lion and make a real difference. She had a backup plan. Rhino did not."

"How does this apply to the real world?" said Mike.

"In our careers, we need to make sure we have options, just like Mongoose," said Denise. "We never know when doing what's right or trying to have an impact will require us to challenge the status quo and expose us to greater risks. Last week, I mentioned that I always keep my resume up to date, just in case I upset someone who can hurt my career. I think that's even more central to this week's story than last week's."

"That's how I see it," said Lily. "As our business environment gets more uncertain, we have to work harder to make sure we have options. Our dependence on a single company for our livelihood increases the pressure to conform rather than speak up."

"Are you saying we need to kiss company loyalty goodbye?" asked Mike.

"Not at all, but I don't see loyalty as committing to the same company for the rest of my life. To me, loyalty means doing my best to add value to my employer for as long as I collect a paycheck. In reality, my company is free to eliminate my job at any time it sees fit. That's their right. So I feel free to sell my services elsewhere if I can get a better deal. It's free enterprise in action."

"Isn't that a little mercenary, simply selling your services to the highest bidder?"

Lily shook her head. "Not necessarily. When I say a better deal, I don't just mean money. Really, it's about fulfillment. I might change jobs because I'm bored, or because the opportunities for challenge have dried up. If the company doesn't allow me to work on things that keep me excited, I owe it to myself to look elsewhere. The fact is that if I lose my passion for my work, I'm no longer giving my best to the company. At that point I'm not doing anyone any favors by hanging on. I just don't think loyalty is measured in years of service; it's measured by how much service we put in those years. If I don't feel inspired to give my best anymore, I've got to change things in the job so I *do* feel inspired. And if that doesn't work, I've got to go someplace where I can feel inspired again."

"So you're saying '*change* your job...or change your *job*,'" said Mike. "I suppose both sides maintain the relationship as long as it's mutually beneficial, but I still think I'd wonder about the loyalty of someone who cultivated options just so they could quit whenever they felt like it."

Denise's brow furrowed. "It isn't as much about having options so you can quit any time you wish—it's about having a safety net that makes it easier for you to do the right thing under difficult circumstances.

Remember, Mongoose didn't leave the group when she was in trouble. Her planning enabled her to challenge Lion and stay where she was, unlike Rhino, who was banished. We need options, because having an impact requires that we speak up and take certain risks. Most of us have an innate psychological fear of risk, yet taking none might be the most dangerous career choice of all."

"You're not just talking about major risks, like the one Mongoose took, are you?" asked Lily. "Those kinds of risks aren't very common."

"You're right," said Denise. "I'm talking mostly about the risk-taking involved in everyday decisions. Some people feel so vulnerable, they won't take even the smallest of risks—like the person who has a good idea for improving a work process, but doesn't say anything because it's never been done before, or a subordinate who hesitates to share her creative ideas because she's worried about what her overly-analytical boss might think. I have a friend who's completely bored in his current job, but won't talk to his boss about it. He's worried about her reaction. Having options is the safety net. It makes speaking up easier by reducing the potential downsides."

Carlos nodded. "Exactly. The bigger the risks you plan to take, the bigger the safety net you'll need. And there's no bigger risk than challenging unethical behavior, especially if that behavior involves someone above you in the organization."

"I get it," said Mike. "Fear can take a toll on organizations as well as employees. When we don't have options, we feel like we're living on the edge of a cliff; there's little margin for error, so we become overly cautious. We grow faster when we feel safe enough to experiment with new ways of working and thinking."

"And the more cautious we are," added Denise, "the less we learn. The less we learn, the less value we add. The less value we add, the more vulnerable we are. It's an interesting paradox. When people avoid small risks, they put their careers at even greater risk."

"When you step back and look at all of this," Mike said, "what we're really talking about here is avoiding dependence. Having options makes us less vulnerable because it reduces our dependence. So what else can reduce our dependence?"

"I'd say getting out of debt is a big one," said Lily. "There's nothing that increases our dependence quicker than debt. I've heard it said that 'debt is the slavery of the free.' When we get into debt and live from paycheck to paycheck, we can feel entirely dependent on a boss or a company for that paycheck. Once that happens, we transform from risk-takers to order takers."

"But how can we avoid being dependent on a company for our paychecks?" asked Carlos. "It doesn't feel realistic. Look at me; I've got only one job, and although I don't think I'm in imminent danger of losing it, I'm definitely dependent on my paycheck. I'm not independently wealthy, and neither is anyone I know. So is it realistic to be truly independent?"

Denise leaned forward. "We all need a paycheck. What we don't need is to be dependent on a single company for that paycheck. If my company went out of business tomorrow, I have the skills I need to find another job quite quickly. I don't have any offers in my back pocket right now, and I'm not actively seeking them, but I know I'm employable. If I think about it, getting this MBA is part of my strategy for remaining employable. My company's not paying for this—it's coming out of my own pocket. But the MBA is worthwhile if it keeps me employable. So avoiding dependence doesn't require you to be independently wealthy. It only requires you to be employable."

"I consider myself employable," said Lily, "but even that's not always enough. So I carry what I call unemployment insurance in the form of personal savings. I learned it growing up; my mother was a single mom who got laid off from a management job in Beijing when I was a kid. Finding another job took her eight months, and the only reason we didn't lose our apartment is because she had enough savings stashed away. Having that financial safety net meant my mother didn't need to simply take the first job offer that came her way. She could be selective."

"Good point," said Denise. "Maybe we need to be employable, as well as have some savings to fall back on. Have any of you heard of Mike Martz?"

Mike nodded. "He was a coach in the NFL."

"That's right. Before working for the National Football League, he was fired along with the rest of the Arizona State University coaching staff. Even though he was employable as a college coach, Martz couldn't get a paying job in the pros. So he signed on as an unpaid intern with an NFL team in Los Angeles. He wasn't put on the payroll for almost a year—it must have been a huge financial challenge for his family. There's no way he could've pulled it off if he'd been totally dependent on a monthly paycheck. His financial safety net gave him the time to prove he had what it took to be a coach at the professional level."

"Nice story, but it's hard for me to relate," Carlos said. "College football coaches get healthy paychecks, so building a financial reserve was easy for him."

"Easier than it is for you and me, maybe, but honestly, if I can do it, you can too," said Lily. "You've just got to commit to living within your income."

Carlos grinned. "I can't even live within my credit."

"Maybe the problem is that your yearning capacity exceeds your earning capacity."

"I guess I gotta reign in my urge to splurge! So, Lily, how do you control the urge?"

"We make ourselves poor by trying to appear rich, spending money we don't have on things we don't need to impress people we don't even know. I've always remembered my mom's advice: 'Most people build up debt in good times, then have to pay it off in bad times. Don't be like them. Use the good times to pay off debt and build your financial reserves for the bad times.' I've tried to follow her advice. Though I earn a good deal less than a lot of people I know, I have a lot more peace of mind than they do."

"You still haven't told me how you actually pull that off," said Carlos.

"It's pretty basic stuff. For example, when I buy a car, I buy one that's two or three years old with fewer than thirty thousand miles on it. I pay it off in two years but I drive it for eight or more. When the car's paid off, I put that car payment into a savings or investment account. That way I never miss the money. Like I said—basic."

"It may be basic, but maybe that's what makes it so powerful," said Carlos. "You know, that could actually work for me. The challenge I face is time. It'll take several years for me to accumulate enough for a solid safety net. In the meantime, I'm vulnerable."

"There is a short-term remedy," Mike offered. "Do you have equity in your home?"

"Yes. Are you suggesting I get a home equity loan?"

"No. With a home equity loan you get a check; then you're required to begin repaying it immediately, with interest. I'm talking about a line of credit. It's different. You only draw down the line to the extent that you need to, and only when you really need it. If you never lose your job, you don't have to use the available credit, so you never pay any interest. That way your safety net costs nothing to install and you don't pay anything for it unless you use it."

"Mike's right," said Lily. "But if you're going to apply for a line of credit, be sure to apply now, while you're still drawing a paycheck. That way you're likely to get approved. Be very careful though; you've got to discipline yourself not to use the credit unless you absolutely have to. Tap into it only if you get laid off."

The group summarized their insights:

- **Your confidence to speak up enables you to both maintain your integrity and become a force for change.**
- **Your willingness to speak up and innovate increases in proportion to the number of options you have.**
- **Being employable is the best source of options.**
- **Loyalty is not about tenure. It's about adding value and ensuring mutual benefit.**
- **Manage your finances to avoid short-term dependence on others for that paycheck.**
- **Build a personal financial safety net.**
- **Avoiding risk may be the riskiest strategy of all.**

THE DANGER OF CONFORMITY:
SOCIAL PRESSURE MAKES US STUPID

"If you view life at 50 years old as you did at 20, you've wasted 30 years of your life."

—Muhammad Ali

Some years ago, researcher Solomon Asch told fifty college students they were going to take a vision test. The 50 student were tested one at a time in a room with seven others—none of whom were real participants but actors under the direction of Asch.

Asch would show the room a set of lines and ask which of the three—A, B, or C—most resembled the line on the left, as displayed on the next page. Participants responded out loud in the front of the group. The seven actors went first; the real participant responded last.

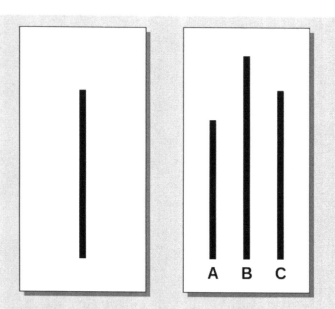

The correct answer is clear: C is the line of equal length. All the tests were similarly obvious, and when participants were asked to give their answers in private, they were wrong less than 1% of the time.

When participants had to respond in front of the seven actors, however, different results emerged. When the seven actors were all told to give the same incorrect response, the real participant often gave the same incorrect response, even though it was undeniably wrong. Over 12 tests, 75% of participants gave an incorrect response at least once. Only 25% were willing to consistently go against the group's wrong answers.

People bold enough to consistently stand against the crowd are, like Mongoose, in the minority. Deep within our brains resides a bundle of neurons called the amygdala. The Latin root of the word amygdala means "almond," which gives us an idea of its approximate size and shape. It is one of the most important stimulus processors in your brain, and is particularly attuned to motivationally-relevant stimuli, i.e., those stimuli which drive reward or punishment.

The amygdala acts subconsciously and processes stimuli *before* they reach our conscious selves, and it is especially sensitive to fear stimuli. Fear derived from social situations often triggers the strongest amygdala responses of all. Neuroscientist Vachily Klucharev measured brain responses in an fMRI (functional magnetic resonance imaging) scanner and found that when there is a conflict between an individual and the surrounding group, the subconscious will often automatically adjust the individual's opinion to be more in line with that of the group, thus avoiding the risk of punishment from others. Psychologists call this "groupthink," and it usually happens without us even being aware of it.

Humans are social creatures, easily blinded and gagged by our innate desire to get along. Even when faced with explicit, obvious facts, we will often keep quiet in order to maintain social cohesion. This tendency carries over even when faced with matters of life and death. The now-famous Milgram experiments show just how far people sometimes go to avoid rocking the boat.

Stanley Milgram was a psychology professor fascinated with obedience and the lengths to which people will go in order to conform. Participants were invited into a room with a researcher in a white lab coat. The researcher explained that the participant would perform the role of a teacher, and needed to teach word pairs to a participant in another room (the other "participant" was an actor). The participant teacher and the learner in the other room could communicate verbally, but could not see each other. The teacher's room included a control board supposedly wired directly to the skin of the learner in the other room. Each time the learner gave a wrong answer, the researcher told the teacher to send an electric shock to the learner, upping the voltage each time. The lowest setting was "slight shock," the middle "intense shock," and the final setting was "XXX," suggesting an especially dangerous outcome. Before the experiment began, the actor who played the learner told the teacher he had a heart condition.

When the initial shocks were given, the learner complained. As the shocks got stronger, the learner's complaints grew louder and increasingly frantic. The learner would ask to end the experiment. If the teacher hesitated in administering the shock, the experimenter explained that the experiment must go on. As the shocks got stronger, the learner's requests turned to tear-filled pleas. If the teacher used the highest XXX setting, the learner made no sound at all; an eerie silence was all the teacher heard.

Of course, there were no real shocks, but the teacher didn't know that. The teacher was given no additional reward for taking the experiment to its grisly conclusion. With no threat of punishment if the teacher did not follow through, and only a single man in a white lab coat pushing for obedience, the percentage of participants who endured the screams and pleas of the learner and turned the shock dial to the highest possible setting was an astonishing 65%.

Milgram ran many versions of this study. When there was no researcher in the room encouraging them to continue, not a single teacher took the shocks to the highest level. In other words, all that was needed for people to ignore their internal moral compass was an authority figure saying the experiment must go on. Even when the participants refused to continue, none insisted the experiment itself be discontinued. Participants simply asked to be excused. All participants displayed obvious signs of significant stress, yet the majority continued despite the screams and pleas to stop.

Studies like this confirm the critical importance of safety nets. Facing no threat of punishment or promise of reward, the vast majority of participants in Milgram's experiment capitulated in the face of the social pressure from a single authority figure. In the real world, opposing the incorrect or unethical decision of a superior is almost always associated with the added pressure of anticipated negative consequences. If we fear punishment for speaking out — socially, financially, or otherwise — and if speaking out involves going against the wishes of more than one other person, we are even more likely than those in the Milgram study to comply and act against our own conscience.

The importance of courage in a meaningful life cannot be overstated. Aristotle observed, "Courage is the first virtue that makes all other virtues possible." Courage, however, does not necessarily mean an absence of fear or an innate immunity to conformity, but from having a personal safety net, be it financial savings, a highly marketable skillset, or another person fighting in your corner. In his matching-line experiments, Asch found that if just one of the seven actors gave the correct response, the real participants were far more likely to buck the trend and give the correct answer.

Napoleon Bonaparte said, "Courage is like love — it must have hope to nourish it." A safety net gives us the hope we need to be courageous.

"The trouble is, if you don't risk anything, you can risk even more."

—Erica Jong

APPLICATION EXERCISE

Given your insights from this chapter, what can you do to achieve greater self-reliance, self-confidence, and employability?

- **What can you do to build a stronger financial safety net for yourself?**

_____
_____
_____
_____
_____
_____
_____

- **What new skills or experiences will make you more employable?**

_____
_____
_____
_____
_____
_____

- What can you do to acquire these skills and experiences?

  _____

  _____

  _____

  _____

  _____

  _____

  _____

- What risks do you need to take to keep yourself employable and to expand your impact at work?

  _____

  _____

  _____

  _____

  _____

  _____

  _____

"Most of us spend our lives as if we had another one in the bank."

—Ben Irwin

CHAPTER 3
CHICKEN AND DOVE

"Money often costs too much."

—Ralph Waldo Emerson

Professor Khumbulani smiled and opened his arms to take in the entire room. "Welcome," he said, beginning to pace and clasping his hands behind his back. "Today will be a little different. My tee time was cancelled—" he winked at Carlos, whose eyes grew wide, "—so today, we won't break into groups. Instead we'll discuss the story together as a class. This legend emerged toward the end of the 19th century, from the Ashanti tribe, when Ghana was a British colony called the Gold Coast, so named for the enormous gold deposits discovered there."

Chicken and Dove were good friends who spent their mornings together scouring the forest for food. When the day grew too hot for anything but relaxing conversation, Chicken and Dove roosted in the shade and talked.

Beyond a low hill covered in vines, down a winding and dusty path, lay a human village, or kraal. Chicken and Dove had never visited, but they had seen smoke from the cooking fires curling lazily into the sky at dusk.

One day, early in the morning, when the insects were few and grass seeds too small to be of much satisfaction, Chicken and Dove met to reorganize their search. "I'll go to the village," said Chicken, "while you fly up to the forest canopy. Whatever we find, we'll bring back here to share." Dove agreed, and the two went their separate ways.

Chicken pecked and plodded down the path, moving hesitantly toward the village's human-scented boundaries. Poking her head around the corner of a fence, she saw an old man sitting quietly on a stool, his back resting against the wall of his hut. The man noticed Chicken out of the corner of his eye and gingerly held out a weathered hand. His fingers spread to reveal twenty kernels of plump, golden corn. Chicken, overcome, scurried into the open, pecking frantically at the kernels. Soon her crop was bulging.

Just as she turned to leave, however, the old man swooped in. He was swift and light. It happened so fast that Chicken forgot to be afraid. He had picked her up, cradled her carefully, and placed her in a coop made of sticks and twine. The space was small but clean. In the corner sat a red clay dish brimming with fresh water. There was no choice but to settle down and wait.

Every morning and evening, the old man supplied Chicken with plump kernels of corn and juicy leftovers from his meals. Every afternoon he changed her water. Then he spent the heat of the day sitting on his stool, weaving thatch and discussing the events of the village with Chicken.

After many days, Dove discovered her friend's new roost. Peering head-cocked through the bars of the coop, she said, "What are you doing here, Chicken? Why did you not return to the forest?"

"This very kind man has taken me under his wing, so to speak," said Chicken. "He feeds me every day and talks to me as a close friend. I am never starved after fruitless hunts for food. In fact, I am never hungry at all. I have become, I think, someone of great importance to the village." Chicken fluffed her feathers with pride. "What about you, Dove? Are you finding food in the forest?"

"I find enough, but it is such hard work that I'm exhausted at the end of each day. Usually I fall asleep before the sun crosses the horizon."

Chicken clucked sympathetically. "How sorry I am for you, Dove. I wish you could be with me in my house. I wish you could have someone fuss over you and care for you as I do."

Dove had to admit she had never seen Chicken looking so fine. Her feathers shone, her breast was plump, and her eyes gleamed with health. "But aren't you sick of being cooped up? You can't fly. You can't even run. There's hardly room to move. How can I help you escape?"

"Not even an elephant ear filled with fat grasshoppers could tempt me to leave," said Chicken. "Yes, it may be cramped, but I have plentiful food, clean water, and a little old man who fusses over my every cluck. I'll never go hungry again. Just look." Chicken pointed a wing at the man coming down the

path. "Here he is with my mid-afternoon snack. Come visit me again sometime, won't you?"

Dove returned to the forest. That night she slept soundly in the banana palms, her head buried under her wing. The smoke from the cooking fires curled white against the dark sky, accompanied by peals of laughter from the village, but she did not wake. Yet even in sleep, when the smoky, savory smells from the fire reached Dove's nose, her feathers stood on end.

Dove returned in the morning to find the coop empty. Only two white feathers on the floor hinted at the fate of its former resident.

"Oh dear," cooed Dove. "I may never be someone of great importance, and I may have to scratch for my food, but it is clearly better to be free."

Professor Khumbulani's calm, distant gaze returned to the present. At last he spoke again. "The elders of the Ashanti tribe used this story to warn their children about the dangers of living under colonial rule. In the historical-political context of the Gold Coast, who does the old man represent?"

"Could it be the British Crown?" asked one student.

"Indeed. And what specific dangers were the Ashanti children being warned about?"

Lily raised her hand. "I think they were being warned about not becoming too dependent on the British for their everyday survival, about being seduced by trinkets from the British."

"Tell me more."

"If I remember my history correctly, as different parts of Africa were colonized by the European powers, they would sometimes co-opt the local ruling class. The colonial powers made these local rulers feel important, as illustrated in the folktale. The local rulers received special privileges, a few rare manufactured European goods, and the necessities for a more modern life. This dependence made them easier to control, which set them up to become victims."

"Excellent. Our focus today is on the dangers of dependence. Let us pull these lessons from the past into our own world. In the context of modern organizations, how does dependence set you up to become a victim?"

"Well," said a student in the back row, "in our case, dependence probably doesn't involve something as basic as food or water. But, say there's a recession; if I fear losing my job and having to live with my parents again, it may be enough to keep me quiet about things like unsafe working conditions or an abusive boss. I'd feel trapped."

The professor nodded. "It is clearly a dangerous place to be, at least for the individual. As leaders and future leaders in organizations, you also need to understand the cost to organizations. How does dependence hurt organizations?"

"Some people become very passive. I've had subordinates who relied entirely on me for their motivation," complained one young woman. "If I was not constantly acting as their cheerleader, they lost focus. And when they saw a problem, they wouldn't take the initiative to fix it. They'd wait for me to tell them what to do."

"They expect their bosses to make their careers bloom for them," said another. "And when that doesn't happen—or it doesn't happen fast enough—they become disengaged, less productive, and critical of everyone but themselves."

"Exactly," said Khumbulani. "I suspect more than a few of you have had similar experiences. If your goal is to do meaningful work and expand your impact, you need to answer seven questions for yourself. Remember these as you create your personal career plans, which you will give to me at the end of our final meeting:

"First: what do you want out of your career—what's most important to you? Second: what skills, talents and interests make you especially valuable to an employer? Third: what are your company's needs, and what can you do in your current job to expand your contributions to the success of your team or organization? Fourth: what skills do you need to improve to excel in your current job? Fifth: if you are not excited about going to work each day, what can you do to make your current job more engaging? Sixth: what future opportunities or assignments in the organization are a good fit for your unique talents and interests? And seventh: what skills, accomplishments, and attributes will help open doors to the opportunities that most appeal to you, and will help you succeed once you get there?"

After giving time for note taking, the professor continued. "Let us return to the story. What was the basis for Chicken's dependence?"

Carlos jumped in. "On a basic level it was food, water and shelter. But Chicken's dependence went well beyond those physiological needs—she also had a psychological dependence. The old man fussed over her. He made her feel important, even loved. Modern organizations can be equally seductive. I've seen contracts bristling with perks and rewards that go way beyond satisfying material needs."

"Good point. What are some corporate rewards and incentives that make us feel important?" As students began to voice suggestions, the professor wrote them on the whiteboard:

Corporate Incentives and Rewards
- **Larger salaries (along with the status symbols and toys money can buy)**
- **Medical benefits**
- **Vacation and sick leave**
- **Visibility**
- **Status and power**
- **Bonuses**
- **Stock options**
- **Tuition reimbursement**
- **Retirement packages**
- **Life insurance**
- **Ego-inflating titles**
- **Private office**
- **Praise**

Once the brainstorming slowed, the professor put down his marker. "What did Chicken have to give up in order for the old man to treat her like royalty?"

A student near the middle of the room said, "Her freedom to run and fly."

Another said, "In the short term Chicken gave up her freedom, but in the long term she gave up a lot more. She ended up in the pot."

"Yes," said the professor. "Benjamin Franklin said, 'Dost thou love life? Then do not squander time, for that is the stuff life is made of.' Chicken unwittingly gave up the rest of her time on this earth for the privilege of not having to scratch for food. Would any of you argue she made a good trade?"

The class was silent.

"It appears you think Chicken got a bad deal. How about us? When we give 40 or 50 or 60 hours each week to a company, we are trading a significant portion of our waking lives for money—and maybe for a few of those other incentives we listed earlier. What do you say—good trade?"

"Not if you're only getting what we put on the board," said Denise.

"Then what else do we need to feel we have a reasonable deal?"

"I need to enjoy my work," piped a man in the back. "I need to know that what I do really makes a difference. I need the freedom to be creative."

"How many of you share his view?" asked the professor. Most hands went up, and Khumbulani nodded, saying "We can sum it up in one word: Fulfillment. I mentioned fulfillment during our first session, but we did not discuss it. Fulfillment comes from making progress on tasks we consider important, from accomplishing things that really matter—to ourselves and others. Fulfillment tends to last longer than other rewards. And the best thing about fulfillment is that it is non-taxable income. But if we are not careful, the incentives organizations use to attract and keep us can create the mental coops which limit our ability to make a difference—"

"—thereby robbing us of fulfillment," said Carlos.

The professor nodded, smiling, and continued. "When we take a job because it has more status, power, or money attached—rather than because it gives us the chance to make a real difference—we are trading life itself for trinkets."

"Hold on a minute," said Mike. "We're already pursuing careers in big companies because that's where the rewards are. We're getting MBAs to climb higher. It seems like you're equating organizations and rewards with coops that make us miserable. And ironically, these "villains" are paying our tuition and your salary."

Khumbulani's eyes shone. "It is fair to raise that concern. It comes up every year. Please allow me to make two points.

"First, we need to remember that the coops are not the incentives themselves. Neither are the coops the organizations dispensing incentives. Rather, the coops are the mindsets limiting our ability to have an impact, preventing us from realizing our potential, and robbing us of fulfillment. The problem would be easy to address if the organization were the coop: we could leave. But it is not that easy. We build the coops in our heads, and we take them with us wherever we go.

"Second, we are the ones who decide whether or not incentives become mental coops. Eleanor Roosevelt said, 'No one can make you feel inferior without your consent.' Similarly, while an organization can offer incentives, it cannot rob us of our freedom or fulfillment unless we consent to it. One way we give consent is by allowing corporate incentives to make our career decisions. If we aren't careful, we end up with comfortable lifestyles but unfulfilled lives."

"It's not as simple as that," interjected another student. "Incentives aren't just about money or maintaining lifestyles. Some corporate incentives also deliver fun and fulfillment."

"Please, give us an example."

"Take power. I could couple my power with my creativity to direct the efforts of a large group and achieve something that makes a real difference in the world. Power could become a source of fun and fulfillment for me."

"Excellent. Notice you did not talk about power as an end in itself. You framed it instead as a means to a higher end: making a difference. When power and other incentives become ends unto themselves, they can morph into mental traps or career coops. What I'm hoping we glean from this discussion is that we don't have to abandon large organizations to find fun or fulfillment; any organization, big or small, can be a rich source of opportunity and satisfaction. They can help us accumulate the resources and talent which enable us to do far more in this world than we might as individuals. We just have to keep the incentives in perspective."

"No disrespect," said Carlos, "but I've heard that same line from some of the executives in my company."

"What have they said?"

Carlos snorted a laugh. "In short? That they want us to be satisfied with intrinsic rewards, while they load up on all the stock options they can get."

Khumbulani sighed, nodded, and clasped his hands behind his back. "Yes. Some short-sighted executives preach the gospel of intrinsic rewards, while practicing the gospel of self-enrichment. Tell me: What will you do about this inequity?"

"As soon as I'm finished with this MBA, I'm outta there," said Carlos.

"Wasn't your contract bristling with perks?"

"I wish!"

"As I suspected. The consequences of organizational inequity are dissatisfaction and high turnover. And the first employees to leave are the most employable ones. Your name, young man?"

"Carlos Mendez."

"So, Mr. Mendez, why not leave sooner?"

"To be honest, I can't afford to. This is an expensive program and they're paying for it. But when I have that diploma in my hand, I'm gone."

"Is this inequity a major source of frustration?"

"Yes."

"How would you rate your job satisfaction?"

"Mediocre. I'm doing a lot of trivial stuff my boss keeps delegating to me because I happen to do it well."

"Have you raised this issue with your boss?"

"Not yet."

"Why not?"

"Because there are consequences for challenging

your boss, and I don't want to jeopardize my job and the tuition reimbursement that comes with it."

"Seems like these incentives of yours have become a trap. Do you agree?"

Carlos nodded silently.

"So you have found yourself in precisely the mental coop we have been discussing. But do not despair. You are in the right class, because you are going to learn how to regain control of your career. Do you mind if we talk a little more about your situation? I think we could all learn something from it."

"Sure," replied Carlos.

"Let me summarize the situation thus far. Mr. Mendez does not want to give up his tuition reimbursement. On the other hand, he is not having fun at work, does not feel he is given the kind of projects that would allow him to have a real impact, and would leave now if he could. In essence, he has decided that eighteen more months of frustration is a reasonable price to pay to save himself roughly sixty thousand dollars. Good deal? Maybe, maybe not. Only Mr. Mendez can decide. Mr. Mendez believes he cannot afford to give up the tuition reimbursement. At what point did that belief become a coop?"

A new student joined the conversation. "When he decided fulfillment and tuition reimbursement were mutually exclusive."

"That is right. When a belief seriously diminishes our ability to experience fulfillment, or when it prevents us from having a greater impact, it has become a coop."

Lily spoke up. "Sometimes, though, we have to delay short-term gratification so we can reach longer-term goals, like getting our MBAs. That's life. We give up things like leisure time with our families to do this, but we do it because these sacrifices will help our careers for years to come."

"A critical point," Khumbulani agreed. "We all have to make trade-offs between our short- and long-term interests. What is critical is knowing where to draw the line. If we are not careful, we can become what I call serial compromisers. This year, for a little tuition reimbursement, we won't move to a job that might offer greater opportunities to make a difference. Next year, vesting stock options convince us we cannot afford to leave. After the options vest, something else comes along which we are inevitably afraid to lose. The cycle continues. We keep sacrificing today on the altar of tomorrow, but tomorrow never comes.

"A consultant I know, Richard Leider, wrote, 'Remember, there are two currencies that make up our quality of life: time and money. While money can be spent, lost or squandered, and then earned again, time cannot be re-earned. It will eventually run out. Life will end. Opportunities will be gone in the wink of an eye.'

The professors black shoes clicked on the gleaming floor. "Let us get back to Mr. Mendez. How could this dependence limit his ability to make a difference?"

"He could become overly cautious," offered a student in the front row. "If you want to make a difference, you need to be willing to take some risks — a central theme of last week's story."

"Agreed. So let us explore the process whereby our decisions trap us."

Professor Khumbulani paused, shuffled through his papers, then held one in the air. "Here we go. In a recent study, people were asked, 'How much money would you need to earn in order to eliminate your financial worries?' The response? Regardless of income level, it was about thirty percent more. People who earned forty thousand a year said another twelve ought to do it. Those earning a hundred thought another thirty would be enough. See, most people keep moving the goal on themselves. They're chasing a mirage in the desert. No matter how hard they try to reach their destination, it keeps receding into the distance. The never-ending quest for financial security means fulfillment remains on the back burner—at least until tomorrow."

"You seem to be saying that security and financial peace of mind are unattainable," grumbled a student. "I thought one of the things I'd learn in this class is how to achieve a greater sense of financial security."

"For some—many, even—security and financial peace of mind will remain out of reach, but only because people keep moving the goal line on themselves. For those with the discipline to hold the line in place, I think you will learn how to achieve both greater fulfillment and financial peace of mind. That includes you, Mr. Mendez, and, no doubt, others in this room. Thank you for letting us pry into your career. I trust the discussion was helpful for everyone. I certainly hope you found it worthwhile."

"I think so," said Carlos. "I realize I've put fulfillment on the back burner. Time to make some tough decisions. But I wonder how my bosses would react if they knew they were paying you to encourage me to leave the organization."

Khumbulani waved in dismissal. "I am not worried about that. I would suggest, however, that you not make any major career decisions until we finish this series. The coops that trap us are in our own heads and travel with us, so moving to another organization may not solve your dilemma. However, as you develop new insights and apply new thinking to your current situation at work, you will probably decide to stay put. Not because you feel trapped by the tuition reimbursement program or any other incentive, but because you will have learned how to achieve greater fulfillment right where you are. To reiterate, the danger lies not with the incentives, but within ourselves. The trouble begins when we allow incentives, rather than fulfillment, to drive our career choices.

"Let me provide a concrete example of what happens when people put incentive ahead of fulfillment. Several years ago, I taught a career workshop for fifteen managers at a large oil company. Most of them were, shall we say, not enthusiastic about their careers. I asked each of them to share their best career experience with the group, and when everyone finished I asked what themes had emerged from those experiences. One participant observed that fourteen of the fifteen had described an experience that took place prior to becoming a manager. The tragedy was that most of them did not enjoy their current jobs.

"These managers wished they could return to the technical work that had energized them earlier in their careers, but they believed it was too late. Some felt they had lost the technical skills needed to be successful in their previous roles, while others had lifestyles that required the more lucrative financial packages available only to managers. Almost all of them worried that if they resigned from management and went back to their technical roles, they would be viewed as failures."

The professor looked down and shook his head. "They gave up true success for the *trappings* of success. They no longer did what they loved or what they did best. In place of making a real difference and experiencing fulfillment, they accumulated status symbols: bigger offices, fancy titles, nicer cars, and more expensive homes. In essence, these managers forfeited the joy and self-respect that comes to those who control their own destinies."

"Maybe they gave up fulfillment, but they gained greater financial peace of mind," suggested a student.

"I wish that were true, but it did not work out that way. Most of them adopted more lavish lifestyles, so their status in the community mirrored their greater status in the company. Their financial obligations kept expanding to absorb any salary increases, so financial peace of mind was always one pay raise away. Psychologists call it the hedonic treadmill. In a very real sense they had become enslaved by their ever-increasing standard of living. As I said earlier, salary increases only bring greater peace of mind to those who have the discipline to stick to the original goal line.

"There is another source of financial peace we have not yet mentioned: the peace that comes from knowing that because you are the best at what you do, you are highly employable. These managers' satisfaction in their current roles had fallen, and over time they realized that they were not as effective as the managers who *did* find fulfillment in those roles. This discovery made them feel vulnerable, further undermining their financial peace of mind.

"These managers reminded me of another group of people I encountered while working as a volunteer counsellor in a state prison. I concluded that the inmates and managers had at least two things in common: they didn't like where they were, and they blamed others for their predicament. I also concluded that in some respects, the prisoners were less trapped than those unhappy leaders. Unlike the managers, most of the prisoners had plans to escape!"

Students chuckled and Professor Khumbulani continued. "Let me make one thing clear: most of our career problems are self-inflicted. Organizations are not served by burning people out or depriving them of fulfillment. On the contrary, organizations desperately want every employee to be enthusiastic about their work and the opportunity to make a difference."

"Then why do we see so many people unhappy with their jobs?" asked a student.

"The curse of dependence and complacency. Individuals simply leave their career decisions to their managers and the organization," said the professor.

Another student raised her hand. "The people higher up know where the opportunities are, and they have the power to make things happen, so why shouldn't I let them make career decisions for me?"

"There are two problems. First, rarely will anyone be managing your particular career. Second, even if such a wonderful and generous person existed, you still would not want them making those decisions for you. It is not that they would act in bad faith, but that they don't know your unique talents, motivations, and needs like you do. Consequently, if you let someone else make these decisions for you, you're likely to end up in roles which better fit them—not you. That is why organizations need and want people to control their own careers."

"Fulfillment is nice," said one student, who sat with his arms crossed, "but it doesn't put food on my table or pay my bills. For me, fulfillment comes from providing for my family. Money comes first. Personal fulfillment at work is something I'll pursue when I'm wealthy enough to not have to worry about money."

"Thank you for that segue," said Professor Khumbulani, smiling. "Let me introduce you to something I call the Paradox of Incentives."

"In the long run, people who pursue incentives rather than fulfillment usually end up with fewer rewards as well as less fulfillment, just like the oil company managers I mentioned. But those who pursue fulfillment rather than incentives usually end up doing better in both areas."

Several students looked skeptical. One asked, "Is this a theory you've invented to freak out MBA students, or is there some research supporting it?"

"I'm glad you asked, because I do have data—and if what I just said freaked you out, this might completely push you over the edge. Feel free to step outside for the next few minutes if you're not sure you're ready—if this will be a trigger for you."

The students laughed nervously but none moved. The professor crossed the room and switched off the lights. Late autumn sun filtered through the windows. The professor closed the blinds, then wheeled from the corner an old overhead projector. "What's that?" asked one student, much to the amusement of some. Most had never seen such a contraption.

"Something we used before computers conquered the world," said the professor with a smile. "Some time ago, fifteen hundred college graduates were asked a question about how they chose their careers. This is that question." Khumbulani switched on the projector. The question was splayed in white light on the screen:

When you began your career, which of the following two descriptions best summarizes why you made the choice you did:
Option A—I chose my career to make money now in order to do what I want to later.
Option B—I chose my career based on what I want to do now and I'll worry about money later.

"Of the graduates, about eighty percent said 'Show me the money!' More specifically, 1,245 identified Option A while only 255 chose Option B. Researchers then followed up with the graduates twenty years later to see if there was a correlation between financial success and how they chose their careers. Here is what they found."

For Love or Money?		
	Group A:	Group B:
Criteria for selecting career	Chose career "to make money now in order to do what I want to later." n=1245	Chose career based on "what I want to do now, and I'll worry about money later." n=255
Percentage who were millionaires 20 years later	1%	29%

"Now for the million-dollar question, pun intended: Why did those who focused on fulfillment end up, on average, with more wealth than those who went for the money?"

Denise said, "Those who went for money ended up in jobs they didn't really like. The lack of passion probably translated into mediocre work."

"That is right. The theory and the data are in alignment, proving the adage that there is nothing more practical than a good theory. When you love your work, it is fun. It is energizing. It sparks your creativity, and you are likely to do it much better than those who are in it for money alone. When you do something better than most others, you have a greater impact, and the market will pay a premium for that. On the other hand, when you do work you do not love, it becomes a chore. It drains you, and you are unlikely to do it very well.

Because the market seldom pays a premium for average work, your income is likely to be average."

"I'm not sure that's always the case," argued Mike. "My father is a linguistics professor who loves his work, but he's never made much money pursuing fulfillment. In fact, I have a higher salary after only five years in the workforce than he does after thirty years of dedicated service."

"It is true that some professions do not pay as well as others," responded the professor, "no matter how good you are. That is why seventy-one percent of Group B were *not* millionaires. A number of them were school teachers, nurses and social workers. So if you want to test the connection between fulfillment and finance, you cannot compare university professors to Wall Street bankers. You have to compare university professors against university professors in the same field. From that standpoint, I am confident you would find that, on average, those professors who love their work will do better than those who become professors just because they like the security of tenure."

"You may be right," Mike replied. "My father does seem to be more successful than most of his colleagues at snagging research grants. For a university professor, having money to pursue your research interests is a big form of compensation."

"It certainly is. I am happy that we are now thinking about incentives more broadly. And thank you for raising the issue.

"To summarize, we build our own coops. We build them by how we think and how we make our choices. Organizations can certainly foster environments that either support or undermine a sense of freedom. However, true freedom comes from within, when we keep incentives in perspective and make career decisions in line with who we really are.

"Before we end today's conversation, I would like to talk briefly about the term 'free agent.' Based on what we have discussed today, what would it mean for someone to be a free agent in the corporate world?"

"Someone who doesn't abdicate her career decisions to the organization or to her boss, and who is assertive in moving her career in the direction she chooses," said Lily.

"How about someone who jealously guards his freedom to choose by reducing his dependence on the organization," said another.

"I think I've got it," said Carlos. "A free agent doesn't buy into the political slogan, 'It's the economy, stupid.' The free agent's slogan is, 'It's the fulfillment, stupid.'" Most of the students smiled, except for some who realized they had chosen their current jobs primarily to make money.

"Those are all good observations. Next time, we will take a look at the notion of career engagement, and revisit what it means to be a free agent. See you then."

Carlos remained seated as everyone filed out of the room. His attempt to lighten the mood a moment earlier had been his way of acknowledging that up to this point in his life he had allowed money too much weight in his career decisions. After 45 minutes of scribbling down ideas, Carlos opened his laptop and created two flowcharts. The first he called The Downward Spiral, to capture his career journey up to this point. The second he called The Upward Spiral, to define his future path.

The Downward Spiral

Conditioned by society (media, family, friends, school), or because of concerns over personal security, I equate money with success.

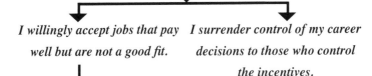

My career decisions are based first and foremost on financial considerations. I choose to worry about fulfillment later.

I willingly accept jobs that pay well but are not a good fit.

I surrender control of my career decisions to those who control the incentives.

I enjoy a comfortable lifestyle, but feel trapped and frustrated at work.

Those who control the incentives know a lot less than I do about what would be a good fit. Their decisions (along with my own) limit my ability to contribute to my full potential.

Despite my conscientious efforts, my performance is not quite as good as the performance of those who chose their jobs based on fulfillment and fit.

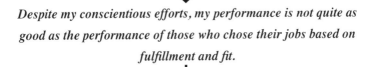

Those in control of the incentives notice the performance gap, and over time my opportunities and rewards are undermined.

The Upward Spiral

*I make career decisions based on fit and fulfillment
first, and choose to worry about incentives
(including money) later.*

*I feel good about myself because I do what I do best and
make a difference in this world.*

*I retain control of my career decisions. (I do not surrender
power to those who control the money and incentives —
because money and incentives are not my top priority.)*

*I make my own career decisions, and ensure my
assignments are a good fit with my talents and interests.*

*This leads to greater fulfillment, motivation
and productivity at work. I'm able to give my best, which
shows in the results I achieve.*

*My rewards and future opportunities in the organization
are expanded. Consequently, sustainable fulfillment and
financial peace of mind are more certain.*

FULFILLMENT:
THE NEUROSCIENCE OF HAPPINESS

---

*"Choose a job you love,
and you will never have to
work a day in your life."*

—Anonymous

When the authors first discovered the story of Chicken and Dove, they saw it differently than the MBA students did in their discussion. The authors saw it primarily as a story warning us about the dangers of staying in the (supposedly safe) cage of our own comfort zones. Chicken assumed that happiness came from security above all else. Dove assumed freedom was more fulfilling than security. But what leads to real happiness and fulfillment for us humans?

To begin, it's worth pointing out that fulfillment does not mean we experience good feelings and satisfaction all the time. People can be very happy with their life overall while feeling sad or anxious or angry at a particular moment. For the purposes of this discussion, we will use the terms happiness and fulfillment both to mean long-term life satisfaction.

Considering how ravenously the human race drives itself toward making more money and consuming more goods, we might conclude that money is the real source of happiness. The reality is more nuanced.

First, the authors are not those annoying types who say money doesn't buy happiness. If your money isn't buying you happiness, you're spending it wrong! A robust body of research has shown that money does buy happiness...until your basic needs are met, after which it doesn't make much difference at all. In the United States, a yearly pay increase from $20,000 to $50,000 would have a measurable and long-term impact on that person's happiness. But a jump from $100,000 to $500,000? This increase will deliver a short-term bump in happiness, but virtually no difference in terms of long-term happiness. Breaking free of poverty delivers significant satisfaction. Moving from middle-class to wealthy does not. (We know that as you read those numbers, you're probably skeptical. You believe you'd definitely be happier if you experienced that $400K salary boost. And for a short while, you would. But, as decades of lottery winners have taught us, the happiness boost doesn't last long).

Once basic needs are met, there are strategies for spending money that can lead to small bumps in happiness. Research shows that memories gained from spending money on experiences generally provide more—and longer-lasting—fulfillment than spending money on physical goods. If you are struggling to choose between the latest HDTV or the great vacation, the great vacation will likely lead to a larger and more enduring increase in happiness.

When we do choose to spend money on things (we cannot live by experiences alone), science tells us how to maximize our fulfillment there as well. We tend to be happier if we spend our money on those things we use most often and for the longest periods of time. So spend your money where you spend your time. If you don't spend much of your day in the car, but you do spend a lot of time in front of the computer, avoid splurging on the car. Buy a vehicle that will reliably get you where you need to go without bursting into flames, and splurge instead on an exceptional computer and top-notch software. The computer you use for eight hours a day will have a far greater impact on your mood than a car you use for a 30-minute commute. You spend a lot of time in bed every day, while spending comparatively little time on the toilet (hopefully). Spend your hard-earned cash accordingly.

There's an even better option: spend your money on someone else. Interestingly, the vast majority of people say that if given $1,000, they

would be happier if they spent it on themselves.
Yet when actually given the opportunity to rate
their own level of happiness, it is consistently
higher when they have used money on others.
This holds true even for those who rate
themselves as above-average in selfishness. The
effect remains in poverty-stricken countries like
Uganda; when experiments were carried out there,
those who spent the money on others still reported
themselves as happier than when spending the
money on themselves, despite often not having
enough to meet their own basic needs.

Finally, avoid debt. Debt can cause significant
stress, which is a death knell for happiness. Utilize
debt only when absolutely necessary, and pay it
off sooner rather than later.

Since money is among the weakest tools for
increasing our happiness, let's talk about much
more powerful tools for driving fulfillment. The
first two on the following list are beyond our
control, but the rest we can change:

1. **Be either young or old, but not in
   the middle.** Those in their late sixties
   consistently rate themselves as happier
   than those of any younger age group.
   Contrary to popular belief, growing old is
   a happy thing.

   There is another happiness peak:
   around our mid-twenties. Happiness

bottoms out at middle age, then consistently goes up from there. Depending on where you are in your life, this may be very pleasing—or deeply depressing—news.

Curiously, when asked which group is happier, both older folks and younger folks point to the younger group, even though the older folks consistently scored higher on happiness assessments. Our perceptions regarding the comparative happiness of others is notoriously unreliable.

While working on the final draft of this very chapter, one of the authors came down with an antibiotic-resistant double ear infection that temporarily robbed him of his hearing and eventually required surgery. Less than thirty days later, the same author experienced a lumbar spinal disc herniation that made it almost impossible to walk for weeks. He is especially gratified to know that despite his recent medical challenges and desire to return to the indestructible body of his twenties, his happiest days are still ahead.

2. **Be born with a happy brain.** In every Indo-European language, the word for happiness shares linguistic roots with the word for luck. Whether we like it or not, the luck of our genes plays a significant

role in our own happiness. Half or more of our baseline level of happiness is programmed into our genes, which then (mostly) determines the unique neurochemical milieu in which our brain will be swimming for the rest of its life.

Some people are simply naturally happier than others. If you are old enough to be reading this book, you will have a pretty good idea of where you might fit. If you weren't born with the genes to be blissfully happy on a regular basis, don't be too hard on yourself or give up in despair. If others consistently seem to display more happiness than you, don't let that be a concern. Recognize that some of it is beyond your control; it is the result of your personal genetic lottery. We are not left powerless, however. Points 3 through 10 below provide a number of actionable ideas for increasing happiness, regardless of age or genes.

3. **Keep fit.** Aerobic exercise is a powerful way to boost happiness. Aerobic exercises—those that get the heart pumping like running or swimming— release endorphins, which is the brain's primary happy chemical. (Anaerobic exercise—like lifting weights—does not have this effect, though it is beneficial

in other ways.) Exercise also decreases stress and boosts both confidence and the immune system.

Please note that being *fit* does not mean being *thin*. A doctor or health specialist can work with you to determine what fitness means for your particular age and body type.

4. **Get plenty of sleep.** Every hour of sleep leads to an approximately 5% increase in reported happiness upon waking. But only up to a point—after 9.5 hours of sleep, happiness actually drops. (This is only true on average. Because each individual's sleep needs can differ significantly, you may choose to experiment with different periods of sleep to find out what works best for you. Most people need between seven and nine hours of sleep per night.)

5. **In a bad mood? Think of something that genuinely makes you smile.** Then let yourself smile. It used to be thought that our moods affected our physical behaviors (which they do), but that it didn't work the other way around. The latest research suggests otherwise. Physical behaviors feed back to the brain and actually alter its mood. If we smile, that indicates to our brains that we must be happy right now. It then releases hormones to bring us closer to the mood that the body is acting out.

Use your body to trick your brain into a happier frame of mind. (This only works if it is a genuine smile. Researchers found that if people fake smiled, their mood actually worsened. So think of something happy, or of someone you love, to get that authentic smile.)

6. **Socialize.** Even those who label themselves as introverted—and even those who struggle with social anxiety—rate themselves as happier on days they spend quality time with friends and family than on days they isolate themselves.

Both authors of this book, while outgoing, are also introverted. After a party or stimulating conversation over an extended dinner, they both go home and hide from the world. Because socializing is mentally exhausting, they recharge by interspersing their social activities with adequate periods of time alone. But they are still happier on days they spend some time with others than on days they completely withdraw from society.

The research supports this. In fact, the quality (not quantity) of one's social connections is one of the best predictors of happiness that has yet been measured. To make this effect even stronger, surround yourself with mostly happy, optimistic, caring people. Steer clear of cynics, chronic complainers, and people who lack empathy. We tend to become more like those around us, so choose your social circles wisely.

7. **Help others.** Brains love to ruminate. They will obsess—over the future, over the past, over any little thing—to the point of driving us into depression or anxiety or exhaustion or all three. Getting out of our own heads by focusing on serving those around us is not simply a nice application of the Golden Rule; it's a great boost to happiness and fulfillment.

8. **Cultivate an attitude of gratitude.** This is more than some syrupy slogan. Research has shown a strong correlation between our levels of happiness and the amount of gratitude we show. It also boosts the happiness of the recipient.

    Gratitude does not require another person to work its magic. Keeping a small journal, with a daily list of three things for which you are grateful, will lead to a measurable increase in your happiness.

9. **Do what you love as often as you can, and make much of what you love productive.** Consuming is fun, but only in measured doses; even the most ebullient film fanatics eventually grow weary of watching movies all day.

While our brains get tired of consuming even the most pleasurable things, they appear to have a nearly limitless passion for producing something considered worthwhile. If your work gives you lots of money but little opportunity to do what you love, you will be less happy than those whose work gives them just enough money but lots of what they love.

The claim that happy people are more productive has merit, but it is more accurate to say that productive people are more happy. We will explore this topic further in the next chapter.

10. **Create a sense of control.** Our brains feel significant anxiety if they think they can't control their own environment. Find ways to control events around you—even if that control is illusory—and you will find your happiness increases. For example, you may not be able to control what traffic is like on your way to work, but just by choosing in advance what music or podcast you will listen to while driving will give your brain a sense of control and make the drive more pleasant.

In the end, there is some truth to Chicken's valuation of security. Fulfillment can be very difficult to find if we are constantly nagged by feelings of financial uncertainty. Live within your means and get out of debt, then do everything you can to avoid the gilded cage of dependence.

What's obviously a cage to others might not be so clear to those of us living behind the bars, so we also need a good friend or family member who, like Dove, can warn us about those things we can no longer see. Dove really did have the right idea: fulfillment comes more from freedom—from being in control of one's own destiny—than from any other source.

"The supreme value is not the future but the present. Whoever builds a house for future happiness builds a prison for the present."

—Octavio Paz

APPLICATION EXERCISE

Given your insights from this chapter, what can you do to break free of your own career coop?

- **Which of your existing ideas, beliefs, and habits cause you to surrender control of your career to others, thereby diminishing both your impact and your fulfillment at work?**

_____

_____

_____

_____

_____

_____

_____

- **What new ideas, beliefs, and habits should you adopt in order to retain control of your career, expand your impact, and increase your fulfillment?**

_____

_____

_____

_____

_____

_____

_____

- What are you already doing that you should continue doing to keep control of your career, expand your impact, and increase your fulfillment?

_____

_____

_____

_____

_____

_____

_____

*"There is only one success:
To be able to spend your
life in your own way."*

—Christopher Morley

CHAPTER 4
SCHOOL FOR THE ANIMALS

"Nobody can teach you how to sing the blues. You have to feel the blues."

—Ernestine Anderson

It was a crisp Tuesday evening when the class met for the fourth session of *Engage Yourself*. Professor Khumbulani said, "Before we look at the next folktale, I would like to tie up some loose ends from last week, beginning with what it means to be a free agent.

"First, free agents believe that if you do not enjoy your work—if you are not having fun—the price of your paycheck is too high. Unlike Chicken, free agents are not seduced by the trappings of success. They keep their eyes on the real prize: fulfillment.

"Second, free agents understand that to be the best, one's work must fit one's talents and interests. Free agents know that if they are the best at what they do, the market will pay a premium for their services.

"Third, free agents see themselves not as employees, but as independent business people selling their unique talents and services to an organization. They are the CEOs of their own one-person corporations. When free agents make career decisions, they look inward for direction rather than upward.

"Fourth, free agents view their employers as customers, and understand that the key to staying in business is exceeding their customers' expectations.

"In order to discuss free agents further, let us define engagement." Professor Khumbulani displayed a slide:

Career Engagement: A state of high productivity, fulfillment and growth. Exhibiting the qualities of vigor, drive, confidence, endurance, employability and resilience.

"Fifth, free agents maintain their engagement by making decisions that keep them true to themselves, to their talents and values and interests. They agree with Oscar Wilde who said, 'I don't want to make a living. I want to live.' Free agents recognize that if all you do is make a living, you have lived but half a life. Because free agents are unique in terms of their talents, values, and interests, you will find them at all organization levels. Some free agents remain in technical positions throughout their careers. Others choose the management track. Free agents who go into management don't do it because they're flattered by promotions or attracted by perks. They become managers because they have a talent and passion for getting work done through others; they sense that management roles allow them to do what they do best. Free agents recognize that management is a lot like spandex. While it can theoretically be worn by anyone, it is not a good idea for most.

"Sixth, free agents recognize that their security cannot depend on their employment contract, the stability of their current employer, their current job description, or the whims of a particular boss. Rather, they recognize that responsibility for their security rests squarely upon their own shoulders. Because they never allow their survival to depend on the fortunes of organizations or the favors of bosses, free agents feel free to choose jobs that offer the best fit."

"Seventh, free agents realize that in a changing environment, their employability depends less on what they have done in the past and more on what they can do in the future. Consequently, they put more stock in being learn*ers* than in being learn*ed*. This means free agents don't wait for the company to give them the training they need to remain employable. Like many of you in this class, free agents use their own time and money to keep themselves competitive.

"In summary, free agents attach great importance to achieving both fulfillment and financial peace of mind. But they realize that to achieve both, they do best to focus first on fulfillment.

"After today's folktale, I shall leave you to work in your original groups, but I do have a confession; although this parable involves animals, it does not originate from African folklore. It is taken from an essay by Dr. R. H. Reeves, an educator in the United States. But it is so good I can almost imagine a tribal elder on the Serengeti gathering the youth around the fire to tell this tale."

Once upon a time, the animals decided they must do something heroic to meet the problems of a "New World," so they organized a school. They adopted an activity curriculum consisting of running, climbing, swimming and flying. To make it easier to administer, all the animals took all the same subjects.

The duck was excellent in swimming—better, in fact, than his instructor. And he made excellent grades in flying, but he was very poor in running. Because he was slow in running, he had to stay after school and drop swimming to practice running. This was kept up until his webbed feet were badly worn and he was only average in swimming. But average was acceptable in school, so nobody worried about that except the duck.

The rabbit started at the top of the class in running, but had a nervous breakdown because of so much make-up work in swimming.

The squirrel was excellent in climbing, until she developed frustrations in the flying class when the teacher made her start from the ground up instead of from the treetop down. She also developed cramps from overexertion, resulting in a C in climbing and a D in running.

The eagle was a problem child, and had to be disciplined severely. In climbing class, she beat all the others to the top of the tree, but insisted she use her own way to get there.

At the end of the year, an abnormal eel who could swim exceedingly well and also run, climb and fly a little, had the highest average and was valedictorian.

The prairie dogs stayed out of school and fought the tax levy because the administration would not add digging and burrowing to the curriculum. They apprenticed their children to the badger and later joined the groundhogs and gophers to start a successful private school.

Lily grinned. "This is the best story yet—I really relate to it. A few years ago, I was offered a promotion in Shanghai involving sales to the U.S. It wasn't really what I wanted, but the money was great and my boss asked me to do it. So I did. The move was fun but the job was a disaster. I hated sales. My distaste for it meant I didn't do it very well, which made me like it even less. Such a vicious cycle."

"What did you do?" asked Denise.

"In the end I boiled it down to three options: quit and go to another company, grin and bear it and hope things would get better, or ask for my old job back."

"What about training?" said Carlos. "If you weren't good at it, I'd think training would've helped you get better. If you were properly trained, you might have enjoyed it more."

"I did try training. Lots of it. It didn't work. I was like the duck; training was about as helpful as putting running shoes on webbed feet. It didn't make me run faster. No matter how hard I tried, I was still awkward when it came to selling. My mind just wasn't wired for it. Going to work became quite stressful. Eventually, I plucked up the courage to ask for my old job back."

"You're the duck with pluck," Carlos said, pointing

at Lily with his pen and winking. "But seriously, that must have been a tough decision."

"Professionally, it was the toughest thing I've ever done, mostly because I worried about what my colleagues would think. Would they say I was running away from a challenge? That I was a failure? Yet within hours of asking for my old job I knew I'd made the right choice. Almost instantly, I felt excited about my work again. Plus, rather than thinking less of me, some colleagues told me they really admired what I'd done. They wished they had the guts to push against jobs that weren't a good fit. Instead of moving me back to Beijing, I was sent to the new offices in Germany. It was one of the best experiences of my life."

"I'm glad it worked out," said Denise. "At the same time, I think we've got to weigh that with our organizations' needs for flexibility; not every job can be a perfect fit. Also, we seldom discover all our talents unless we're willing to go beyond our comfort zones."

"Agreed," said Lily, "but we've got to be strategic about how we do it. For example, trying something new in a volunteer capacity or on a part-time basis gives you a low-risk way to discover whether or not it's a good fit. And if it's not, you can easily reverse course without damaging your credibility."

"You know, I can relate to Lily's experience," said Mike. "Career success comes more from building on talents than fixing weaknesses."

"How do you do that?" asked Carlos.

"For starters, I only take jobs that are the right fit, and avoid those that aren't. That was Lily's point.

Then, I build on my talents by developing skills that are supported by those talents."

"What's the difference between a talent and a skill?"

"Let me give you an example," said Mike. "If I had a talent for learning foreign languages, I'd be able to learn, say, Mandarin or Arabic very quickly. But I'd still need to acquire the skills associated with that language, like vocabulary, grammar, usage, and pronunciation."

"So talents are innate and skills are learned. Are you saying that if you build on your talents, you can ignore your weaknesses?"

Mike shook his head. "No way. Let me clarify what I mean by a weakness. A weakness is not the same as a skill deficiency. A weakness is the absence of a talent. Let's face it—ducks are not designed to run, and rabbits aren't designed to swim. On the other hand, if I have a talent for languages but don't speak Russian, is my inability to speak Russian a weakness?"

"Based on your definition, it's a skill deficiency."

"Right. Now, if all you lack is a skill, by all means develop it; you'll be building on your talents. But if you're like the rabbit and lack the talent for swimming, no amount of training or positive mental attitude will turn you into a highly competitive swimmer. Training and practice may make the rabbit proficient enough to avoid drowning, and that may be all the rabbit needs, but trying to turn the rabbit into a star swimmer is a waste of time and effort. I think forcing everyone into the same mold is a recipe for mediocrity. To me, that's the main point of today's story."

"Isn't that being a little defeatist?" asked Denise.

"I don't think so," said Mike. "In fact, this raises one of my pet peeves. I get so irked by motivational speakers who drone on about people being anything they want to be as long as they try hard enough. Whenever someone tells me nothing is impossible, I tell them to lick their eyeball."

Denise grimaced, and continued. "Even if one has a talent, it still takes work—and many stumbles along the way—to develop a skill to a level that makes you world-class. Beethoven may have had some basic talent to start with, but without thousands of hours of study and dedicated practice, few would have heard of him. Isn't there at least some merit to the idea that we can do anything—within reason—that we set our minds to?"

"Maybe some, but only under certain conditions. For example, if someone has a hidden talent for the thing she aspires to do, a positive mental attitude helps by encouraging her to get out of her comfort zone, and getting out of her comfort zone in turn helps her discover that previously-hidden talent. On the other hand, if there's no hidden talent, the results of blind persistence are just blisters and failure. To add insult to injury, while she's trying to become great in an area that's inconsistent with her talents, her true talents take a hit, just like the duck ruined his talent for swimming by focusing so much on running."

"Amen to that," concluded Carlos. "If at first you don't succeed, try, try, and try again. Then let it go. You don't want to look like an idiot."

Denise smiled. "You two may have a point. In my undergrad classes, we learned that people who

consistently fail at work pay a heavy psychological
price. They either burn out or give up. But even if your
overall job is a good fit, you'll still have some duties
that are inconsistent with your talents. Then what?"

"Then I manage my weaknesses instead of fixing
them," said Mike.

"What exactly do you mean by 'manage'?"

"One option is to avoid jobs where being a top
performer requires talents I don't have. As long as my
talents fit the core eighty percent of my job, I can deal
with the other twenty percent."

"But doesn't it limit your growth to stay in your
comfort zone?"

"Not at all. It's critical to distinguish between
talents and skills. Although I deliberately look for
new jobs that fit my talents, I also look for jobs where
I have some significant skill gaps. A new job is only
worth taking if it makes me stretch. That keeps the
work interesting, keeps me out of the comfort zone, and
keeps me employable."

Denise furrowed her brow. "It's still not clear to
me how you manage the twenty percent that doesn't fit
your talents."

Mike smiled. "I partner with people who have
talents that compensate for my weaknesses. That's
another way to manage, rather than fix, weaknesses. I
think people should be themselves."

"I'm not sure I fully agree with that," said Carlos.
"Given some of the people I work with, 'Be yourself'
is the worst advice you could give!" He smiled. "I do
agree with building on strengths, but I'm not entirely

sure about partnering. I think there are situations where managing weaknesses through partnerships can be dangerous."

"Like what?" asked Mike.

"Well, dynamics at work are constantly changing. Partnerships change. People move. Quit. Get fired. Once, I became overly dependent on a teammate who had great complementary talents, but when she got promoted to another part of the company I found myself in deep trouble. There wasn't anyone else to partner with who had the talent I lacked, so I worked at fixing my weakness, and it served me quite well."

"Was your weakness relevant to your core job?"

"Not in terms of time, but definitely in terms of impact. I work in a lab environment. My talents include analytical thinking and creativity, which suit the job well, but it also requires me to sell my ideas to others. I'm not so good in that department, and if I can't sell my ideas, I don't get the resources I need to test or implement those ideas. This sometimes demands that I give presentations, which is definitely not one of my talents. Realistically, presentations take no more than five percent of my time, but they are vital because if I don't do them well, most of my ideas will never make it out of the lab. That five percent can make or break the ninety-five percent where I'm strong, so I've spent a good chunk of time over the last few years developing my presentation skills, and it's really worked."

"How did you develop those skills?" asked Lily.

"First I got some training. Then I looked for every chance I could to practice and get feedback. I even joined Toastmasters, if you can believe it. Right now, I'm probably average when it comes to presentations, but average is good enough to get my managers to loosen the purse strings. If I hadn't worked on that weakness, I think my talent and effort in new product innovation would have been wasted."

"That's a good point," said Mike. "So what we're saying is that while it's critical to have a network to draw on, becoming dependent on a single person can make us vulnerable; there are times, then, when we should work on our weaknesses. Even in those cases, we probably only want to do that if the weaknesses are undermining our ability to use our talents."

"I have something that's worked for me," said Lily. "When I run into stuff I have to do but don't enjoy, I try to restructure things. For example, I love technology but I hate dealing with details. My current job has a lot of routine details, so I wrote a simple software program to automate the routine. That left me with more time for what I truly enjoy."

"Which raises another issue," added Mike. "You said you hated details. You didn't say you weren't *good* at details. There's a real danger in being good at things you don't enjoy."

"Why's that?" asked Lily.

"The mixture of recognition and opportunity is seductive. It's hard to leave a job you do well, especially when your boss and your customers are singing your praises. I'm good at numbers but they bore me to tears. If I look at people who have achieved phenomenal success in their chosen fields, they've all had talent as well as a passion for their work."

"That makes sense," said Lily. "Talent without passion quickly runs out of steam. And passion without talent produces average results, which leaves you feeling discouraged. I think true genius only emerges when talent is ignited by passion. When we find work that fits our genius, that's when we really shine."

"I like the word genius," said Carlos. "Problem is, someone once said, 'While genius has its limits, stupidity knows no bounds.'"

Lily stifled a grin and said, "Your point?"

"No point," replied Carlos. "Seriously, though, what I want to know is why organizations continue to overlook the value of matching the genius of individuals with the tasks at hand. Why do they try to get everyone to fit the same mold?"

"As the story put it, it's easier to administer when everyone is interchangeable," Denise said. "It isn't realistic to expect organizations to figure out the best fit for every employee. One message of this class is that finding the right fit is each individual's responsibility. We've got to figure out our own genius, then influence our organizations to assign us roles where we can make a significant difference. If we choose not to influence the system, everyone loses. We experience less fulfillment at work, and the company is left with under-motivated and under-productive people."

"Even if we try to influence the system," added Mike, "the system may not be flexible enough to meet our needs. Or, if I have a talent and passion for a task that doesn't add much value to the organization, it may not be in the organization's interests to meet my needs.

If that's the case, I may have to move to a company where that task is highly valued—just like the prairie dogs and gophers did."

"Which brings us back to the issue of dependence raised in the earlier parables," Denise said. "If we don't have options, we tend not to question the system. Like the duck, we do whatever we're told, regardless of the lack of fit. In the end, everyone loses."

"Right," said Lily. "And I can see another link to the dependence issue. When we do work that's foreign to who we really are, we're unfulfilled. We try to fill that emptiness with material things and get ourselves deeper in debt, but it never compensates for what's missing. In the end we're even more dependent on the company for that paycheck, and we still feel empty."

Everyone nodded, looking at their shoes. Carlos piped up with a suggestion, "Speaking of empty, isn't it time to go eat?" They smiled, agreeing.

The team quickly summarized their insights on being free agents:

- **Manage your career as a business and treat your employer as a customer.**
- **Maximize your engagement by seeking opportunities that are (1) aligned with your genius (i.e., talents and passions), and (2) require you to stretch.**
- **Figure out where your genius lies. Then influence the organization to put you in roles that fit.**
- **Focus on managing rather than fixing your weaknesses:**
  - **only take jobs where the core 80 percent is a good fit.**
  - **partner with people who have the talents you lack.**
  - **structure or restructure your work to minimize the impact of your weaknesses.**
- **Only try to fix weaknesses when they prevent you from fully utilizing your talents.**
- **If you let others manage your career, you will end up like the duck. Control your own destiny.**

OUR AMAZING, LIAR BRAINS:
THE DANGERS OF THE COMFORT ZONE

"The great aim of education is not knowledge, but action."

—Herbert Spencer

The human brain is composed of approximately 86 billion neurons, with literally more connections between them than there are stars in the Milky Way galaxy. Of those 86 billion neurons, over ninety percent are subconsciously controlled, humming happily without any explicit direction from our self-aware, conscious selves.

We like to think we are in charge of our brains, but in reality, we only have direct control and conscious awareness of a few billion of our own neurons. If our subconscious brain wants to do something, it's going to do it, often without telling the conscious brain (i.e., us) what it's up to.

Our brains are enormously energy intensive. Though the brain weighs a mere 3 pounds, it consumes roughly 20% of all the body's energy, even when at rest. Because food was not always readily available to our cave-dwelling ancestors, the brain adapted to minimize its energy use. If it can coast, it will. If it can avoid using the smart but high-energy prefrontal cortex—the seat of our complex reasoning and self-awareness—it will. And sometimes, if we feel we've lost control of our environment, many of the brain's higher functions slow to a crawl or shut down entirely. This caused problems for the duck and it can cause even greater problems for us.

The effect is called learned helplessness. If we believe we've lost control, we surrender to what we perceive as the inevitable in order to conserve energy. It's the same reason so many people don't vote: they do not believe it will change anything. That is a form of learned helplessness.

In one study, a scientist named by Martin Seligman, (who, contrary to what the following might suggest, actually gained his fame as a happiness psychologist), inflicted a community of rats with fatal tumors, then split them into two groups. One group was given electric shocks but could press a lever to escape. The other group was given shocks but no method of escape. One month later, sixty-three percent of the rats who could escape the shocks had rejected their tumors; the cancer was gone. Of the rats who could not escape, only 23% rejected their tumors. Learned helplessness can have a powerful physical effect.

When the authors discuss The School for the Animals story with clients in career management workshops, people sometimes ask, "Why would

the duck allow that to happen? Why wouldn't
he leave rather than let the school destroy his
swimming ability?" There are three possibilities:

Dependence, as discussed among the students
in Khumbulani's class, is the first.

Learned helplessness is the second. Learned
helplessness plays out in the workplace with
unfortunate regularity. If we feel we have no
control, our brains simply take us down the
path of least resistance. We become passive and
follow along, like the duck, even if we are certain
something is not in our best interests. As long as
we think we have no control, we will be right.
Thanks to learned helplessness, our brains trick us
into surrendering even when it isn't necessary.

The third possibility is the status quo bias.
Because we like to feel good, when we feel stuck
in a bad situation our brains trick us into thinking
it's not really so terrible. If your job is so boring
it could be successfully marketed as a sleep aid,
if your coworkers would lose a game of checkers
with a chimp, or if your boss is from the very
depths of hell, your brain will pump you up with
soothing thoughts to keep the depression at bay.
"Oh, it's not so bad. Let's just keep doing what
we're doing. At least we're not stuck with Jill's
job. That one's truly awful."

The brain does this even when faced with
matters of life and death. When natural disasters
threaten, many people assume things will keep

going as before, underestimating the probability of the disaster occurring, as well as its impact. For example, even with advanced warning of a life-threatening hurricane heading their way, many people remain in their homes, confident it can't really be as bad as experts warn.

John Leach, at the University of Lancaster, found that seventy-five percent of people react in this way when faced with a catastrophic event. The brain will latch onto the statement of a single expert who claims the hurricane will be less serious than predicted, while simultaneously dismissing the opinions of nine experts warning of a potentially catastrophic storm. People say to themselves, "I don't care if that's what most experts say. I've lived here 40 years and we've never had a serious hurricane. The news programs are blowing things out of proportion to boost their ratings." If the brain can cause us to downplay clear evidence of a looming catastrophe, how much easier it is for the brain to trick us into thinking that the evidence pointing to a rapidly sinking career is a temporary anomaly, and everything will turn out just fine.

To avoid these neural traps, regularly challenge yourself to do something that falls beyond your day-to-day status-quo behaviors. Do you teeter on the shy side of the scale? Then force yourself to strike up a conversation with that new employee at work. Are you scared of heights? Go bungee jumping. Do you find it hard to express your feelings verbally? Have an open, honest conversation with a loved one. The more practice you have breaking free of your own comfort zones, the greater your sense of control, and the easier it becomes to embrace change and new opportunities.

Beware your brain's tendency to follow the path of least resistance. Beware learned helplessness and the status quo bias. Change, though scary, is far more preferable than rotting in a meaningless job for years. (The topic of change could fill an entire chapter by itself. In fact, it will, in the very next section.)

"Hard work beats talent when talent doesn't work hard."

—Tim Notke

APPLICATION EXERCISE

Given your insights from this chapter, what can you do to take greater control of your career and utilize more of your genius at work?

- **What talents do you possess that you would like to use more in your current job?**

  _____

  _____

  _____

  _____

  _____

  _____

  _____

- **What weaknesses are preventing you from fully using your talents? Which of these should you work on and which should you manage? How?**

  _____

  _____

  _____

  _____

  _____

  _____

  _____

- How can you influence your supervisor to use you in ways more consistent with your talents?

  _____
  _____
  _____
  _____
  _____
  _____
  _____

- What can you do to avoid learned helplessness and the status quo bias?

  _____
  _____
  _____
  _____
  _____
  _____
  _____

"The world is more malleable than you think and it's waiting for you to hammer it into shape."

—Bono

CHAPTER 5
THE BEAR WHO DARED

---

*"Most people live and die with
their music still unplayed.
They never dare try."*

—Mary Kay Ash

"This next story is one my father used to tell to
me as a child growing up in Zululand," said Professor
Khumbulani, sitting, relaxed, in a wooden armchair
at the front of the room. No one knew whether he'd
brought it with him. None asked. "It explains the
origins of the human race. According to this folktale,
it is not humans and apes who share an ancestor—it is
bears who are most closely related to humans."

*Two young bears, Ilanga and Igwala, were facing
their first winter away from home. They had been born
to the same mother, at the same time, in the same den,
but they were as different as fish and fowl. Igwala
always stayed close to his mother's side, while Ilanga
would run ahead, looking to explore. Igwala ate
nothing but berries and small fish his mother caught*

for him, but Ilanga would lick the hide off a hippo if she thought it would taste good.

One late autumn day, Ilanga and Igwala sat in a berry patch near their cave, eating all they could see. A long winter sleep lay ahead, and they needed to grow fat before cold arrived. As they ate, the sky darkened with boiling storm clouds. Suddenly, lightning forked across the sky, striking an old, gnarled tree near the mouth of their cave. The tree shattered in a cloud of sparks. The stump that remained burst into flames, orange and yellow and red, like the colors of the leaves.

Ilanga and Igwala had never faced fire before. Igwala hung back, not sure what to make of this unfamiliar entity. Ilanga ran straight for it, stopping only when she felt the heat of the flames sear her coat. Calling for her brother to join her, she lay down by the fire's warm glow. Igwala nestled in behind his sister, and the two delighted in the fire's soothing flicker.

They spent that night under the stars, warmer outside than they had ever been in the cave. Ilanga thought, "Wouldn't it be wonderful if we could keep this little sun? We wouldn't be stuck all winter long inside that ugly cave."

The next day, as the flames grew smaller and the air grew colder, the bears grew worried. "Little sun," they pleaded, "give us more warmth. We are growing colder and each day the sky gets darker. Shine for us as you did last night."

From the dying embers of the fire a weak voice replied, "Give me wood, and I will give you warmth."

"No," said Igwala, "you must first give me warmth and then I will give you wood."

"Impossible," replied the fire. "If you want more warmth, you must give me more wood."

"I don't remember ever seeing my mother doing that," Igwala thought. "This cannot be a good thing. I am a bear. I must do what bears do and bears do not do this." With that he turned and lumbered slowly toward the damp, dark cave, where he remained until spring.

Ilanga, being of a different mind, chose to do as the fire asked. She would feed it, even though tradition had no place for such behavior. Although her instincts screamed to retreat to the cave, she picked up a broken limb and tossed it atop the dying embers. Just then a small breeze wandered through the camp and the fire sprang back to life. Ilanga quickly learned that when she fed the fire, it gave her heat, and so the cycle continued all winter long. She spent her days tending to the flames and sleeping in its warmth.

Ilanga began to change. Never again did she return to the cave. With the heat of the fire, her heavy fur coat became superfluous. Her hair grew thinner and thinner until most of it disappeared. With all the extra time awake, and the challenges of maintaining the fire throughout the winter, Ilanga learned critical thinking and complex reasoning. She grew in wisdom and eventually became the first of our human race.

Mike spoke first. "When Igwala refuses to give the fire more wood until the fire gives him more heat, it sounds absurd. But just last week a subordinate said to me that he would like to add more value at work, but couldn't until he was given more responsibility. I tried to explain that until he added more value he wouldn't get more responsibility, but he didn't seem to get it. Maybe I should tell him this story."

Carlos looked at the floor. "I hate to admit it, but lately I've been a bit like Igwala myself. A few weeks ago, I complained to my wife that my company doesn't seem to value me as much as it used to, so why should I push myself to give more? After listening to this story, I realize how self-defeating that attitude is. Unless I push myself to go above and beyond, the organization isn't going to value me any more than it does now."

"It seems there are two issues here," said Denise. "First, the warmth of the fire is a metaphor for the rewards we want from organizations. It represents more opportunity to make a difference, or more challenge, or more responsibility, or more respect, or—in my case—more money. And second, organizations are set up like the fire. You've got to make more contribution before it distributes more rewards."

"Something else the story illustrates is that breakthroughs often come only when you're willing to break with tradition, which means you've got to stick your neck out," Mike said. "The people who know exactly when and how to break old rules are real assets to organizations, while those bound by traditional routines can become liabilities."

"That doesn't seem right," said Carlos. "Not all routines are bad. Many are essential for efficiency."

"Think about it in relation to something like job descriptions. The people who hold my team back are those who look at their job descriptions like crystal balls that will lead them safely into the future. In reality, job descriptions just tell us what's been done in the past—not what's needed for the future. So in that way, they're part of traditional routines. If that's all people do for the company, it won't be long before we're out of business."

"Are you saying job descriptions are worthless?"

"Not as long as we see them for what they are," said Mike. "They represent what worked in the past for a specific slot in the company. But competitive advantage seldom comes from replicating the past. Advantage comes from finding new and better ways of doing things. In today's environment, detailed job descriptions are probably outdated by the time they're published."

"If that's true, then what purpose do they serve? Wouldn't organizations be chaotic without job descriptions?"

"Yes and no. Job descriptions don't set the bar for contribution. They simply establish the baseline. They're a starting point for discussions between the employee and supervisor. You shouldn't ignore your job description, but neither should you see it as set in stone. My job description can evolve as I gain new skills and as the company's needs change."

"And it evolves best when we take the initiative, rather than waiting for our bosses to ask," said Lily.

"The people I know who really make a difference are rarely constrained by job descriptions," added Denise. "They don't discard them, but they definitely find ways to go beyond. If you were to rate these people on energy and fulfillment, they'd be off the charts."

"Absolutely," said Mike. "Just last week, I heard about someone who works for the ad agency my company uses in San Francisco. He used to be called a creative assistant, which basically meant he ran errands for the people who made the ads. Then, one day, he came up with an idea for an ad for one of his firm's top clients. He took a risk and went straight to the CEO, who loved the plan. So did the client. The ad turned out to be a great success. This young guy now has a new title, a bigger salary, a private office with a view of the bay, and a much more interesting job. Going beyond his job description changed his life."

"I can accept that to really make a difference you need to go beyond your job description," said Carlos, "but what happens if an organization fails to live up to its side of the bargain? Sometimes people go beyond their job descriptions but get nothing in return. They add more wood but don't get more heat."

"That's true," agreed Mike. "In the short term, inequities often exist. But there's a good reason why the formal reward system has to lag behind the individual's contributions—at least a little."

"And why's that?"

"It's just good business practice. As a manager I don't raise someone's salary the moment they do something new. Since it's almost impossible to take away a raise after it's been given, I want to be sure the higher level of contribution is sustainable. So I hold back on the raise until there's enough evidence of permanent change. People have to take a leap of faith, just as Ilanga did, and act on the theory that their efforts will be rewarded."

Lily frowned. "People will take that leap of faith, but if the formal system never catches up, or if the delay is too great, some will start withholding the wood to restore balance. The most employable people will take their talents elsewhere. Either way, the organization loses. So, although I agree with Mike that leaders shouldn't be too quick to give out salary increases, they do at least need to recognize those short-term bumps in contribution."

"Something like a one-time reward or bonus would do the job" said Carlos. "I agree with Lily that it's in the company's self-interest to recognize their people in a timely way, but sometimes they don't. And if you don't get either the raise or some kind of bonus, you're just another sap who's been exploited."

"Not necessarily," said Mike. "In the process of doing something different, you're likely to learn new skills that make you more employable—and you may even get to add a significant achievement to your resume. In today's environment, that's worth a lot."

"I hadn't thought of it that way," said Carlos. "So what can we do to ensure we get both the learning and the recognition, or at least keep the lag between contribution and reward as short as possible?"

"Find subtle ways to make your contributions more visible," replied Denise. "For example, if a customer writes you a thank-you note, find a way to get it into your supervisor's hands—although it's usually best if it goes directly from your customer to your supervisor. You can also make use of Einstein's notion that our theories determine what we see."

"How does that work?"

"Psychologists call it confirmation bias: we tend
to look for information that supports the views we
already hold, and ignore information that counters
our established beliefs. If your supervisor expects
you to do only what's within your job description,
they're subconsciously programmed not to look for
any contributions outside those boundaries, so they're
likely blind to things you do that go beyond your job
description. The trick is to draw their attention to your
additional contributions without making a big fuss."

"That sounds like the old proverb, 'Early to bed,
early to rise, work like hell and advertise,'" said Carlos.
"But advertising could really backfire if it comes across
as a crass attempt at self-promotion."

"One way I've found to avoid that perception is
to talk about it *before* rather than after the fact," said
Denise. "Let's say I'm planning to improve a work
process. I first share my intention with my supervisor,
and then I ask for her feedback. This not only helps
me improve those ideas, but also allows me to plant a
thought in her head that says, 'Denise is about to do
something out of the ordinary.' Now she will be looking
to see what happens, and will probably ask me from
time to time how things are working out. That way,
I don't have to toot my own horn, and I've created a
legitimate reason to keep her informed."

"On top of that," added Mike, "all supervisors want
to know what's going on within their area, so you've
given them one more reason to appreciate you. What
Denise suggested reinforces something else I appreciate
as a supervisor: I place a premium on subordinates who

not only give me what I ask for, but find ways to give me what I didn't know to ask for."

"Now you're talking in riddles," said Lily.

"Take Post-it® notes," said Mike. "When the inventor, Art Fry, created the prototype and started selling his idea within 3M, nobody was asking for the product. But he had recognized an unarticulated need, and that's what made Post-its so successful. Competitive advantage doesn't come from meeting a customer's spoken needs, because your competitors can easily to do the same thing. But when you identify and meet *un*spoken needs, you really differentiate yourself from the competition. It gives you an edge. As a supervisor, I can't possibly identify all the needs of our customers, so when a subordinate sees a need that I've missed and satisfies it, they really stand out."

"But what do you say to people who complain they're already overworked trying to deliver what's expected?" asked Carlos. "They think it's unrealistic to do more."

"In my experience, people can be overworked yet underutilized. That happens when they're in roles that don't take advantage of their strengths. Remember the school for the animals from last week? That lesson fits here too. When people are in roles that don't match their talents—like the duck who had to run and was kept out of the pond—people have to work twice as hard just to keep up with colleagues who are a good fit for the job. On the other hand, when their talents match their jobs, they're much more productive, and going beyond what's expected becomes very realistic."

"Another reason some people can't keep up is stagnation," said Denise. "They're like Igwala who chose to stay in his cave. They keep doing things the way they've always been done. Instead of sharpening their skills or streamlining their processes, they waste time being inefficient. It's a catch-22: They use old, inefficient methods because they don't have time to invent new ones, and they don't have time to invent new methods because the old ones are so inefficient."

"How do you get off that treadmill?" asked Carlos.

"When I feel like I'm on it—that no matter how hard I run, I can't seem to get ahead of my work—I bite the bullet and invest my own time. It may take a few sixty-hour weeks, but in the end it's worth it. Once the new system is up and running, I enjoy my work more and feel a lot less stressed."

"What I'm getting from this," said Carlos, "is that neither poor nor outstanding performers actually meet the expectations in their job descriptions. Only average performers do."

Everyone agreed. They'd been so engrossed in their conversation, they hadn't noticed that the professor and most of the other students had already left.

The team settled on seven principles:

- **You have to take more responsibility before you'll be given more responsibility.**
- **You can't achieve breakthroughs without breaking tradition.**
- **Neither poor nor outstanding performers meet expectations. Only average performers meet expectations.**
- **Nothing truly great happens in any organization until someone goes beyond their job description.**
- **Even when a system is unfair and recognition is limited, adding more value is likely to be rewarded with greater employability. So always seek out ways to add more value.**
- **Create positive expectations in your supervisor's mind about the additional value you plan to add; share your goals and seek your supervisor's input on ideas.**
- **Don't simply meet your supervisor's or your customer's spoken needs. Identify and meet their *un*spoken needs.**

IT'S HOW WE'VE ALWAYS DONE IT: WHY WE LOVE WHAT WE'VE ALREADY GOT

"The most effective way to cope with change is to help create it."

—L.W. Lynett

In 2004 students at Baylor University were asked whether they preferred Pepsi or Coke. (Although the two drinks are virtually identical chemically, people have curiously strong preferences toward one over the other.) They were then given Coke and Pepsi in unlabeled cups. Next, while tasting these sugary delights, participants' neurological responses were measured in an fMRI (functional magnetic resonance imaging) scanner, which allows researchers to see which parts of the brain are most active when engaged in a particular activity.

While tasting the two unidentified drinks, the participants' ventromedial prefrontal cortex (vmpfc) lit up, an indication of pleasure. After tasting both, the drink that got the greatest response from the vmpfc was also the one they said tasted best. No surprises there.

Then the fun began. When participants who preferred the taste of the brand that was *different* from what they declared their brand preference to be, researchers pointed out this fact: "Earlier you said you prefer Coke, but the unlabeled cup you just selected as your favorite was Pepsi." As soon as the participant heard this, their vmpfc actually dampened the response to the unlabeled Pepsi until it was lower than their response to the Coke; the conscious experience of pleasure was subconsciously lowered. At the conclusion of the test, these participants insisted they were wrong before and that they preferred the Coke after all.

This is a fascinating result. The participants' loyalty to their previous preference was so strong that their brains actually altered their perception of pleasure once told which drink was which. Our brains jump through remarkable hoops to prevent us from realizing, even to ourselves, that our preferences may be different than we think.

Our brains have a natural aversion to change, even with something as unimportant as a switch from Coke to Pepsi. This may be due to our illustrious ancestry. In prehistoric times, change was more likely to kill us than help us. So we learned to stick with what we knew. "We've always done it this way, and it never killed us, so we should continue to do it this way." As we see from the soda study, this choice is often made on a subconscious level.

Another player in our curious aversion to change is the endowment effect: we subconsciously attach more value to something we own than to something we don't. You can see this effect in action if you have ever bargained for an item from an individual (rather than buying it in a store). What you think the item is worth is one thing, what they think it's worth is consistently higher, and there's a gap that must be bridged if a sale is to be made. This doesn't happen because we are cheap or the seller is trying to fleece us, but because each person genuinely sees the item as having a different value depending on whether or not they own it.

Psychologists like to give research participants gifts that aren't worth much. In one study, scientists invited participants to discuss how much they would pay for a particular water bottle. Eventually the group reached an average of $5. Some of the participants then received that water bottle for free. At the end of the study, researchers told the water bottle owners, "We'd like to buy that bottle from you. How much do you want for it?" The average response: $8. It became more valuable the minute they owned it.

This is as true of ideas as it is of physical objects. As soon as we presume to own an idea—because we believe in the idea or use it regularly—we assume it has more value than it really does. This makes us even more resistant to change, because change challenges the value of the idea we hold so dear. The bear Ilanga had to let go of her old ideas before she was able to find the greater value of the new idea.

So it is in our careers. Remember, we are going to overvalue anything we think we own, be it a work process, a belief, or information. So the next time you think your existing plan is better than a new plan someone has suggested, resist the temptation to just keep doing what you're doing. Instead of immediately creating a mental list summarizing the advantages of the status quo, write down as many arguments as you can in *favor* of the new idea. If you can't come up with many, ask someone to brainstorm with you. Create another list of the disadvantages to the way things are *currently* done. Carefully read both lists. This will help you counter the endowment effect and open your mind to new ideas.

Simply recognizing that this bias exists within us is a great way to avoid it and to better see the real value in change. If you would like to see concrete examples of this bias in your own life, consider keeping a change journal. Every time you make a change, voluntary or not, record it in your journal, along with how you feel about the change. Revisit that entry in a year and update the record with a summary of how things have gone since, and how you now feel about the change. You'll find that in the majority of cases the change proved to be far more valuable than assumed in your original assessment.

"Change is the law of life. And those who look only to the past or present are certain to miss the future."

—JOHN F. KENNEDY

APPLICATION EXERCISE

Given your insights from this chapter, what can you do to add more value at work?

- What traditions, beliefs, or habits do you need to let go of in order to add more value?

_____

_____

_____

_____

_____

_____

_____

- What are the customer's or the organization's unspoken needs? What are the unspoken needs of your team?

_____

_____

_____

_____

_____

_____

- What can you do to expand your contributions beyond what is in your job description?

  _____
  _____
  _____
  _____
  _____
  _____

- What support will you need from your supervisor in order to expand your contributions? What can you do to get that support?

  _____
  _____
  _____
  _____
  _____
  _____
  _____

_____

"A mind stretched by a new idea never goes back to its original dimensions."

—Oliver Wendell Holmes

_____

CHAPTER 6
WHY ZEBRAS DRINK
WITH BABOONS

"Prejudice is the reason of fools."

—Voltaire

"Zebras are beautiful," said Professor Khumbulani, "and rank high on the lion's list of favorite foods. The Angoni tribe tell their children this story about survival in a highly competitive environment."

Years ago, when grass was plentiful and rains came with comforting regularity, zebras roamed in great family groups. Wandering the endless sea of swaying grasses, passing through the shadows of towering rain clouds, the herds made their way back and forth, up and down, across the Serengeti. And ever following, the lions, who at first took only foals when the zebras stopped to bend and drink from the river, but who in time grew so bold as to take even full-grown adults.

One summer, a curious young zebra noticed the dwindling numbers in her family group. Many of her cousins failed to return from the riverbank. She saw also that the baboons had thrived, their band growing larger as summer progressed. "It doesn't make sense," she said to her mother. "Baboons are smaller and slower than we are. How is it possible that lions catch more of us than they do baboons?"

Her mother said, "If you were a lion, wouldn't you want to eat the most graceful animal on the plains? Look at your brilliant stripes, your fat haunches. Look at the way your belly rounds out like the blossoming of the moon. We are the most desirable creatures upon which the kings of the Serengeti could possibly feed. But the baboons? Have you ever seen such awkward and ugly creatures? Sometimes they run on two legs, sometimes four. No self-respecting lion would bother to chase a baboon; there's no glory in catching such slow and uncoordinated creatures. Only the old, mangy lions go after baboons, as I'm sure you've noticed."

The young zebra had not noticed, but kept it to herself. She was unsatisfied with her mother's response, so she went to her father. Then she went to her aunt. Then she went to her two young uncles who were nearing adulthood and about to leave the herd. To each she asked the same question and from each she received the same reply: "Because we are the most beautiful and graceful creatures on the plains. Because there is no glory in catching a creature as bumbling and graceless as a baboon."

It seemed to the young zebra that she was doomed to become a lion's meal merely because she was fast, graceful, and had the most beautiful coat on the Serengeti. Surely, life could not be so cruel.

One morning, after getting her fill at the river, she looked up to find a large, grizzled old baboon drinking beside her. The zebra's mother was right. He was the definition of ugly. But despite his advanced age, he had also avoided being eaten. Gathering her courage, she turned to him. "Excuse me, sir baboon, but why is it that you and your kind never die in the jaws of lions?"

Ugly though he was, the old baboon was gracious in his reply. "Well, young miss, over the years we've devised a plan which works well for our kind. When we need to drink, a few of our strongest lads climb the tall trees around the waterhole to look for danger. As long as our sentries are silent, we can drink in peace, but when we hear them barking, we run for the trees, as we know our enemies are on their way. Thus it is we stay alive to drink another day."

At last the young zebra understood the secret of the baboons. They avoided the lions' claws not because they were ugly or awkward or equipped with flaming red and blue bottoms, but because they were cunning and wise. It took two full seasons before the young zebra could persuade her family to learn from the baboons, but learn they did. That is why, whenever you see a troop of baboons drinking at the water's edge, the zebras are never far behind.

"So who are the zebras and who are the baboons?" asked Carlos.

"This is really an 'us' versus 'them' story," said Lily. "The zebras are us and the baboons are them."

"The zebras' attitude bothers me," said Denise. "All but one of them assumed they couldn't learn from those 'lesser' animals, just because they could run faster and more gracefully. In psychology, I learned how often we subconsciously choose to favor our own 'kind.' We're just like the zebras. Instead of looking for objective truth, we justify ourselves by placing ourselves and the qualities we already have in the most positive light. It also helps us feel better about ourselves."

"Yeah," said Carlos. "We place a premium on things we do well—like running—and downplay things we don't do well—like climbing. So whatever I do well, I consider critical to the team's success, but the things *you* do well are not nearly as important."

"There's some truth to that," Mike said, "but I'm not sure it's always a case of people deliberately distorting reality to make themselves feel better."

"Most people don't do it deliberately," said Denise. "It's just the way we're wired at a subconscious level."

"Whether it's a conscious or subconscious decision isn't the point for me. I just don't think we do this to make ourselves feel better. A more practical explanation is that it takes less energy for me to associate with people who share my background and interests and values. Then I don't have to worry about someone misinterpreting what I say or taking offense. I don't have to walk on eggshells or start from square one every time I need to explain something I'm doing."

"You're right. Working with a diverse group does take more energy. And because our subconscious brains are programmed to conserve energy whenever they can, they tend to nudge us towards those who share our views and away from those who we're likely to disagree with."

"So if it's subconscious, how do we change it?" asked Lily.

"Conscious effort," said Denise. "A few years ago, we had a partner in my firm who was a real pain in the—well, let's say he was arrogant. I didn't want to work with him, but on some projects I had no choice. It took a lot of effort on my part to work well with that guy, but in hindsight, I learned more from him than from any of the other partners. Also, our disagreements often led to solutions that were more creative than either one of us could have developed alone. Because of that experience, I frequently remind myself of the benefits of working with people who are quite different from me, which has made it easier to consciously push back when my subconscious leads me away from people who see the world differently. On one level, we're genetically programmed to see conflict as dangerous, but on another I think we can reprogram ourselves to view conflict as nature's way of providing a learning opportunity."

"That's helpful," said Lily. "I used to work with composites to build stronger, lighter aircraft components. This is an oversimplification, but essentially you create these components by combining two or more materials with significantly different physical or chemical properties. The combination of carbon fibers and resin result in a product with properties that exceed those of either constituent material. Interestingly, when constructing high performance components, you have to keep the resin-to-fiber ratio down to somewhere between 50/50 and 50/60, to get the optimum combination of lightness and strength. And if you want to optimize the strength over the length and breadth of the component, the trick is to layer the material so the direction of the fibers keeps changing, creating forces in the compound that work against each other. If the layers all had the fibers going in the same direction, the overall integrity of the final product might be compromised."

"So what you're saying is partnering with people who go against your grain is actually a good thing," said Carlos. "And the most effective partnership is where the partners have roughly equal influence."

"Exactly."

"I agree that conflict can be a source of learning and creativity," said Mike, "but only if people know how to deal with it. I remember attending a diversity workshop that suggested we needed to understand our differences so we'd have fewer misunderstandings and less conflict, so we learned about cultural differences and how to be more sensitive to them. Although I discovered how to avoid some unnecessary conflict, I didn't get to where you guys have gone with this folktale."

"And where's that?" asked Lily.

"That we can't just be aware of and sensitive to our differences. If we want to maximize our contribution to the team's success, we must take advantage of others' unique, and sometimes maddening, ways of viewing the world. While I understand the logic in this, it still won't be easy to break my habit of hanging out with people who see things the way I do."

"So when you interview prospective employees, how easy is it to hire people who don't share your strengths or view of the world?" said Denise. "What does valuing diversity mean to you as a leader?"

"It's hard, which probably means I don't do it well."

"I think there's something we've ignored," said Lily. "This story isn't just about people gravitating toward their own kind. It's about blatant prejudice. The zebras didn't just prefer their kind. They created derogatory stereotypes to justify looking down on baboons. Even though my English vocabulary is strong, my Chinese accent sometimes makes it difficult for people to understand me. Some people think I'm less knowledgeable, just because I pronounce words differently or a little more carefully. If we're going to leverage differences, we have to confront our own prejudices as well as challenge the prejudices of others, just like the zebra did."

Carlos nodded. "Thomas Jefferson once said, 'We resort to ridicule when reason is against us,' which is why the zebras bad-mouthed the baboons. The young zebra had to confront the herd with reason before they would even question their prejudice. That's never easy to do, and it doesn't happen quickly."

"Yes, prejudice is a big problem in some organizations," said Mike, "Perhaps most. But I also worry when conflict is automatically blamed on prejudice, on some kind of '-ism.' When two people from the same race or culture clash, we call it an interpersonal conflict. But when two people from different races or cultures clash, it's a diversity problem. Sometimes a disagreement is just a disagreement."

"I've seen that happen," said Lily. "When a male manager mistreats a group of male subordinates, they say he's a jerk. But if a woman does the same thing, she's a man-hater 'like the rest of them.'"

Mike smiled. "Touché! When you think about it, isn't assuming prejudice where none exists just another form of prejudice?"

"You have a point," said Denise.

"Seems we're all guilty of prejudice, even if only on a subconscious level—and it happens with disturbing regularity," said Carlos.

"But why?" asked Lily.

"I think one reason is mental laziness," said Denise. "It comes back to our brains' inclination to save energy. When we can identify someone as part of a group, it's easy to make assumptions about who they are and what they're like, which is a lot easier than taking the time to get to know each individual personally. Unfortunately, assumptions are like termites: you don't see them, but they still wreak havoc. Seeing individuals as representatives of entire groups or classes of people leads to stereotyping, and we need to get beyond that. That doesn't mean we ignore differences, but I've found that once I take the time to really get to know someone of a different background, race, or culture, our differences are almost always overshadowed by our similarities. I'm often surprised how much we have in common. I'm also surprised how different I am from many people who look just like me."

"Viewing an individual as a representative of a group usually hides more than it reveals," said Carlos. "But when structural barriers hurt certain groups, then group identity does become relevant, and these barriers have to be addressed at an organizational level."

"What do you mean?" asked Mike.

Carlos pointed to himself. "If an organization's recruiting practices make it harder for Latinos to find employment there, group identity is a legitimate focus."

"It's also legitimate to suspect prejudice if an individual or manager has a lot of conflict with people from one demographic but not another," said Lily. "Then it's probably not just a disagreement, but something that runs deeper."

"Maybe it is necessary to sometimes look at group issues," agreed Mike. "It's also important to remember Denise's point about getting to know people on an individual level. We shouldn't make the assumption that those who look different will have different values and strengths. Similarly, we shouldn't assume that those who look like us share our values and strengths."

"If I may, I'd like to have the last word on this subject," said Carlos. "The zebra story simply confirms the adage that two heads are better than one—unless they're both stupid."

The group summarized what they learned:

- **Don't allow the premium you place on your own abilities to blind you to the unique strengths of others.**
- **Build diversity into your network. (Don't network only with those who look like you or share your worldview.)**
- **Conflict is nature's way of alerting us to significant learning opportunities.**
- **You will often learn most from people you have the greatest difficulty relating to.**
- **When you are in a position of power, find ways to reduce the power differential so others will be willing to challenge your ideas.**
- **Avoid hiring people in your own image. Build teams with diverse strengths and perspectives.**
- **Avoid stereotyping. Challenge prejudice in yourself and others.**
- **Treat every individual as a unique human being, not as a representative of a group.**

PREJUDICE:
WHY OUR SUBCONSCIOUS IS A BIASED JERK

"It takes a teaspoon of evidence to confirm a stereotype and a truckload of evidence to disprove it."

—Kate Kirkham

The authors of this book are fruits from the same family tree. They both have South African accents, which in some countries are often confused with British accents. As such, they may sometimes sound more intelligent than they really are. This is all thanks to a neurological bias called the halo effect. (Unfortunately for the authors, the effect of their accents do not carry over to the printed word.)

The halo effect is our tendency to judge a person's characteristics and skills based on our overall impression of that person, even when that impression is based on irrelevant attributes. Are you tall? Then you must be more capable than most! (Since researchers began tracking the data, roughly 80% of US presidential elections are won by the taller candidate.) Do you dress well? Then you must take pride in your work! Are you attractive? Then you must also be funny! Add a witheringly-delightful accent to the mix? Then you must be smart! Of course, the accent a person uses bears no correlation whatsoever to their intelligence, yet our brain likes to think it does.

The prefrontal cortex—the critical thinking, self-aware part of your brain—is very smart. But it is also consumes a lot of energy, and is slow and weak when pitted against the subconscious. As Denise noted in the previous discussion, the brain likes to conserve energy. Consequently, it will relegate decisions to the fast but less intelligent subconscious when it can. Judging an individual based on the full range of their personal characteristics takes a lot of time and effort, so the brain takes a mental shortcut. It assumes, based on one or two obvious characteristics, that the person is either good overall or not-so-good overall. It only engages the prefrontal cortex when it needs to or when we force it to.

Attractiveness is an especially powerful halo. Even babies as young as a few days old will stare at an attractive face longer than a less-attractive face. Adults are hardly better. When shown a picture of someone's face, with no other information, participants rate the more attractive faces as more stable, sophisticated, intelligent, successful, and altruistic. Attractive people are also rated as happier and kinder than the general population. Identical essays with different photos attached receive higher scores when attached to photos of more attractive people. Given identical report cards with different photos attached, teachers rated the IQ of the more attractive student higher. More attractive criminals receive lighter sentences to the tune of prison terms that are often years shorter, while criminals without the gift of good looks receive longer-than-average sentences. These biases are generally subconscious.

The halo can work for or against you. And if you are evaluating a new employee, it can easily lead you to make unsubstantiated judgments. Almost 100 years ago psychologist Edward Thorndike discovered this when when he invited commanding officers in the United States military to evaluate their soldiers across a range of characteristics including intellect, neatness, and loyalty. While there is no real-world correlation between someone's intellect and their loyalty, or someone's neatness and their intellect, Thorndike found the commanding officers' rating on the first trait became the basis for their rating on all other traits. If they rated the first trait highly, they were likely to rate all other characteristics roughly as high. If they rated the first characteristic low, they tended to rate the other traits low as well. This happened even when Thorndike warned the officers about the halo effect and instructed them to rate each characteristic independently. Even with explicit instructions, participants just couldn't do it.

These halo effects do not stop at things like height or attractiveness. They include race, gender, age, political affiliation, religion, and a host of characteristics that can lead to danger if not consciously challenged. If unchallenged, it can lead to in-group bias.

In-group bias is especially pernicious because we all struggle with it, yet are usually unaware of its presence and will vehemently deny we are tainted by it. After all, no one wants to be labeled a bigot, and most of us really aren't bigots (at least, our conscious selves aren't). Let's use political affiliation as an example. Have you ever blanketed an entire opposing political party with labels such as "warmongers" or "socialists"? Have you ever wondered why they could possibly believe the things they believe? Do you think that the only reason people have a different affiliation than yourself is because they are less intelligent, less informed, morally bankrupt, or all three? This is an example of in-group bias. We ask someone about one political position—be it healthcare, education, or abortion—and before we have even consciously processed the person's response, our brain will have already decided what kind of a person they are and whether or not we like them.

We do this based on race—even if we have
never had a conscious racist thought, because
bias is subconscious. We do it based on gender—
female musicians who audition behind a curtain
are fifty percent more likely to be selected for
an orchestra than if the reviewers know the
individual playing is a woman—which is true
even if the reviewers themselves are female. Our
brains will go so far as to judge a whole person
based on irrelevant superficialities like skin color
or quantity of hair (yep, there's a bias against
baldness too).

As the example regarding female musicians
illustrates, bias can occur even when a person is
a member of one's own group. Some years ago,
the authors were working on a diversity program
for a client. The training was to be facilitated by
consultants from around the globe. During the
train-the-trainer segment, one of the consultants,
a black gentleman, told us of a recent experience
when his own race-based bias surfaced. As he
boarded the plane to attend this very session
of diversity training, he saw a black pilot enter
the cockpit. This black diversity consultant was
shocked to realize that his first thought was,
"Does that brother know how to fly this thing?"
He had never flown with a black pilot before
and he told us how embarrassed he was to find
himself, if only for a split second, questioning the
abilities of the captain based only on the color of

his skin. Although he consciously dismissed the unfair question as quickly as it entered his head, he realized that despite his background, race, and training, even he was not immune from his subconscious biases.

If left unchecked, these biases can turn into outright prejudice. Bias and prejudice are not the same thing. Bias occurs in the areas of the brain to which we have no direct access. Prejudice occurs when our conscious brain attempts to justify a subconscious bias. This tendency is especially pernicious. Thankfully, contrary to what Carlos stated in the previous discussion, we are not all guilty of prejudice. But we all experience bias, and understanding how prejudice arises from subconscious bias places us in a stronger position to counter prejudice in ourselves.

Even the best of us have biases lurking in our subconscious, but they do not have to turn into prejudice. The question is, do we have the self-awareness necessary to recognize biases when they surface and quickly override them with our more rational brain?

Though the conscious brain is slower and requires more energy, it is far more intelligent than the subconscious brain. Awareness of these neurological shortcuts gives our prefrontal cortex the tool it needs to counter it. If our young zebra had let herself be tricked by the halo effect, or by her in-group bias, she never would have sought to use the knowledge of wise old Baboon. When evaluating the skills of another, be on the lookout for evidence of your own biases at work. Have others (preferably those who tend to see things differently than you) complete their own skill assessments, then compare notes. If you see things differently, ask them for their reasoning and invite them to push back on your assessment. In fact, if you can, make your initial assessment of a new individual by looking at their track record of accomplishments—the outcomes of their work alone—before either seeing the person or hearing their voice. We would be wise not to let our biases get in the way of partnering with people who have skills, perspectives and information that could help us expand our impact at work.

"The problem with conformity
is everyone likes you
except yourself."

—Rita Mae Brown

APPLICATION EXERCISE

Given your insights from this chapter, what can you do to better leverage the strengths of others?

- **What mindsets or practices may be limiting your ability to leverage the strengths and insights of others?**

  _____

  _____

  _____

  _____

  _____

  _____

  _____

- Who can you include to make your professional network more diverse? (Who are the people you tend to disagree with? Who does not share your background or see the world as you do?) If you are in a formal position of leadership, what do you need to do to make others feel comfortable challenging your ideas?

  _____

  _____

  _____

  _____

  _____

  _____

  _____

- What can you do to get to know these people better and learn more from their unique perspectives and experiences?

_____

_____

_____

_____

_____

_____

- Who do you know in your career who may have been a victim of your brain's halo effect or in-group bias? What can you do to avoid making similar mistakes in the future?

_____

_____

_____

_____

_____

_____

_____

"The first problem for all of us—men and women— is not to learn, but to unlearn."

—Gloria Steinem

_____

CHAPTER 7
WHERE ON EARTH
IS TIMBUKTU?

---

*"You make a great mistake
when you suppose that
formal authority is more
powerful than
informal influence."*

—Terence (Roman Philosopher)

"This is the final story in our series," said Professor Khumbulani. "But unlike the previous folktales, this one is all about the humans."

Many years ago, before airplanes and freeways, people traveled across continents by train. The central train station in Johannesburg, South Africa, was the continent's primary transportation hub. Gleaming locomotives arrived from Keetmanshoop, Salisbury, Nairobi, Cape Town, Cairo, and Lorenco Marques.

A team of men, dressed in uniforms with gold-braided epaulettes and shiny brass buttons, serviced the trains. Conductors took tickets, showed passengers to their seats, and turned down the smooth linen sheets in the sleeping cabins. Waiters served travelers in luxurious, brass-guilded dining cars. Porters took luggage—steamer trunks, suitcases, hatboxes, and cages with brightly colored birds—to cabins and baggage cars. At last, loaded, the trains chugged away in a cloud of smoke and squealing steel, crisscrossing Africa in all directions.

One morning, a hardworking porter accidentally dropped a bag belonging to a wealthy industrialist from England. The industrialist was incensed at what he perceived to be the careless treatment of his expensive leather luggage, and promptly launched into a public verbal assault on the hapless porter, scolding the lad, intimidating and humiliating him. Throughout the barrage, the porter stood in the middle of the platform, eyes downcast, offering apologies.

Thankfully, even a self-important boor runs out of steam eventually; the industrialist shoved his hat on his head and stormed to his cabin.

A woman standing nearby witnessed the outburst and approached the porter with commiserations. "I saw what happened there and I've got to tell you, that Englishman was the most vulgar, obnoxious person I've ever seen," she said. "The way he spoke to you was entirely uncalled for. I compliment you on your calm reaction. You kept your dignity, even as he lost his."

"Thank you, ma'am." The porter nodded. "In this job I've learned how to handle abuse. You see, that man is on the southbound train to Cape Town, but his luggage is going north to Timbuktu."

The class laughed. Rather than leave the room, Professor Khumbulani continued. "That is my final story. Because I want to allow time for each team to report on their conclusions, we shall only spend a few minutes on this folktale. What can we learn from it?" "That revenge is a powerful motivator," said one student. "When someone abuses you, grin and bear it while plotting vengeance from behind a smiling mask!" Khumbulani chuckled. "Any others?"

A student raised her hand. "Perhaps the lesson is that we should treat everyone with respect, because you never know who might send your career to Timbuktu."

"Does that mean we only treat people with respect because we think they might hurt us if we do not?"

"Ideally, we respect others because it's the right thing to do," suggested Denise. "But for those people who have a hard time distinguishing between right and wrong, it probably doesn't hurt to remember that what goes around comes around."

"There is a positive side to the idea that what goes around, comes around," added another. "People usually respond in kind. If you treat me with respect, I'll feel obliged to reciprocate."

"And what does reciprocity have to do with building a successful career?" asked the professor.

"For me," replied the student, "career success is about having an impact, and making a real difference is seldom a solo effort. If I want to succeed in my career, I need to work with others and be supported by them. By always respecting others and helping them out when *they* need it, I maximize the chance that I'll get their support when *I* need it."

"Excellent. Reciprocity is the grease of effective organizations. It increases engagement by reducing unnecessary friction and enhancing collaboration. It allows us to have an impact by engaging the talents and energies of those around us.

"Alan Paton, the famous South African antiapartheid author, noted that we should ask ourselves 'not if this or that is expedient, but if it is right.' I believe treating every person with respect is the right thing to do. But if I am honest, I know a little enlightened self-interest helps keep me on the straight and narrow. Now it is time to turn in your reports and share your insights with the class."

Each team took their turn to present their thoughts. Carlos, Lily, Denise and Mike went last. They quickly added one final lesson to their report and called it "Career Laws for the Jungle":

1. **Expand your influence by maximizing the value you create for others. Ignore this, and corporate Elephants will flatten you.**
2. **Make employability your primary source of job security. Options give you the courage to take more risks and to make a real difference, like Mongoose.**
3. **Retain control of your destiny. Do not trade independence and fulfillment for the trappings of career success or you'll end up like Chicken—in boiling water.**
4. **Ensure your talents and passions are engaged by your work, or mediocrity will be your legacy, like Duck.**

5. If you truly want to achieve great things, go beyond your job description and meet the unspoken needs of the business, like Bear.
6. Leverage the strengths of others by building diversity into your network. Be like young Zebra, who learned to partner with baboons.
7. Treat everyone with respect, because reciprocity is the basis for all collaborative relationships. Forget this, and your career might be sent to Timbuktu.

Professor Khumbulani complimented the groups. "I am impressed with the ideas you have identified. If you do what is on your lists, I have no doubt you will avoid the rogue elephants, prejudiced zebras, and dangerous coops that derail careers. And more importantly, you will expand your impact at work and experience greater fun and fulfillment. Let me conclude by putting your ideas into the context of mental constructs or mindsets." Khumbulani sketched the following on the whiteboard:

"Many of your reports were focused on the action side of this sequence. I now want you to focus on your mindsets, which are what ultimately determine your actions. I have prepared a self-assessment. Please complete it now." The professor passed out the assessments. "When you are done, pair up with someone and share your insights." [Authors' note: you can take this assessment yourself beginning on page 174 of this book.]

After the assessments were complete and the discussions concluded, Khumbulani brought the class to an end. "You appear to have uncovered many of the keys to expanding your impact and achieving career success. That is the easy part. Implementing your ideas will be far more important—and more challenging. I wish you all well in this endeavor. Please place your personal career plans on my desk when you leave."

"Before we go," interrupted Carlos with a wry smile, "I have an observation. We've spent these last eight weeks looking for the keys to career success, but whenever I think I've found the right key, they change the darn lock!"

Professor Khumbulani replied, "Then the key to success is to take charge and change the locks yourself."

RECIPROCITY:
WHY FAIRNESS MATTERS

"Those disputing, contradicting, and confuting people are generally unfortunate in their affairs. They get victory, sometimes, but never get good will, which would be of more use to them."

—Benjamin Franklin

Let's play a game.

You and I shall play, and we shall play it only once. A friend has given me $100, which I have been told I must share with you. I can choose to share however much I want. If you accept my offer, we both get to keep our portion of the money. If you reject my offer, my friend takes back the $100 and neither of us gets any money.

This is called the ultimatum game. Variations of it have been used by psychologists and economists for years. So, what amount of money would you be willing to live with? If I gave you $50, or even more, I can be confident you will accept my offer. What if I offer you $40? You'll still be $40 richer, so perhaps you will take it, though you may curse me for my unfairness. But what if I offer you $25? $10? $1?

If I were playing this game with a rational, emotion-free computer, the results would be the same every time; the machine would accept my offer, because any amount of money is better than no money at all. But humans are not, as some economists would have us believe, entirely rational agents. At what amount would you reject free money in order to punish me for my unfairness? Researchers have found that offers of less than thirty percent of the total are usually rejected. Even when the game is played in very poor countries, where $30 might represents one or two weeks' wages, most will reject the offer.

From a purely economic standpoint this is bizarre behavior. If you didn't know I was given $100 to split and I simply handed you $10, you would likely accept it. Just by knowing I received $100 with an obligation to share it drastically alters your likely response. Neuroscientists have found that when faced with an offer perceived as unfair, the brain's anterior insular cortex—an area associated with feelings of disgust—is activated. On the other hand, when someone treats us fairly or does us a kindness, feel-good chemicals like dopamine and oxytocin are released in the brain, which inclines us to react positively toward that person. In other words, we humans are hard-wired to respond negatively if we perceive that we, or those we care about, are treated unfairly. Conversely, we are hard-wired to react positively when others respect us, help us, and treat us fairly.

Because we are programmed with an innate sense of fairness, when something happens that we judge to be unfair, we are willing to punish that unfairness even if we hurt ourselves in the process. For example, in our last story, sending the rude passenger's luggage to the wrong destination could have negative repercussions for the porter if management learns about it.

Revenge is routine in the corporate world. Employees in a computer-chip manufacturing plant might flush expensive product down the toilet to get even with management. A salesperson might choose not to share a critical piece of information with a colleague. The list goes on and on. In the end, we would all be best served by making a commitment to treat others with respect, regardless of their station in life. To quote Malcolm Forbes, the famous publisher from the 20th century, "You can easily judge the character of a man by how he treats those who can do nothing for him."

If we wish to retain the goodwill and support of our colleagues and subordinates, we must not only act in ways that are fair, but also in ways that will be *perceived* as fair. This means that the better we know others—their goals, interests, priorities and values—the more likely we are to make business decisions that will be perceived as fair. Seeking input from others, and being open to their feedback, also helps us make the decisions that will increase feelings of fairness for all parties involved. When making decisions, or designing new policies and systems, always ask, "Who will benefit? Who will be hurt? How can we make this as fair as possible?"

Reciprocity and fairness matter a great deal, which seems so obvious that it feels mildly ridiculous to spell it out. Yet in the real world, our own priorities and emotions sometimes get the best of us, and we forget the importance of fairness and the power of reciprocity.

As the MBA students discussed, reciprocity does not mean we wish to create a "you scratch my back and I'll scratch yours" environment, or that we shouldn't be jerks just because we want people to be nice to us. At the same time, that is how our brains are programmed to assess interactions and we should bear that in mind.

Reciprocity and respect go hand in hand. One key to mastering the power of respect is to discard the old notion that people have to "earn" respect. Rather, accept that every fellow human being is deserving of your respect, at least initially. We all have our own issues and problems, and just because someone has issues or problems that are different than our own does not make them any less worthy of our respect.

"Show respect even to people who don't deserve it, not as a reflection of their character, but as a reflection of your own."

—Dave Willis

APPLICATION EXERCISE

Given your insights from the last chapter, what can you do to build greater reciprocity into your relationships at work?

- **Who are the people at your office who work behind the scenes and seldom get thanked? Who are the people you may be taking for granted?**

  _____

  _____

  _____

  _____

  _____

  _____

  _____

- **What can you do to more effectively communicate your respect for these people? What can you do to show them you appreciate their efforts?**

  _____

  _____

  _____

  _____

  _____

  _____

  _____

- What do you know about the goals, needs, priorities, values and interests of the people with whom you work? What can you do to help them achieve their goals or satisfy their needs?

  _____
  _____
  _____
  _____
  _____
  _____
  _____

- What can you do to make life at work better for everyone? What can you do to improve the climate of reciprocity within your team or organization?

  _____
  _____
  _____
  _____
  _____
  _____
  _____

_____

"The art of being wise is the art of knowing what to overlook."

—William James

_____

CONCLUSION:
WHY THE HUMANS
WROTE A BOOK

"In the absence of reflection, twenty years' experience could be reduced to one year of experience twenty times over."

—Unknown

In a fast-moving economy, your success depends largely on your ability to grow. In turn, your ability to grow depends on your determination to reflect, to question your assumptions and biases, and to identify new behaviors that will unleash your full potential.

We are fortunate to have found careers that make our lives more genuinely fun and fulfilling than we thought possible. We are convinced that if we can do it, so can you. Congratulations on taking the first steps toward becoming a free agent, expanding your impact, and achieving greater fulfillment at work.

To continue down this important path:

- **Share and discuss your insights with others.**
- **Take 5-10 minutes every week for the next three months to review your notes from this book. Identify things you need to change and then do it.**
- **Complete your career plan by answering the seven questions Professor Khumbulani gives on page 66.**
- **Dig a little deeper by visiting www.stepchangelearning.com and explore learning resources that can benefit you and your organization.**

Wishing you fun at work and fulfillment in life,
Michael-John Bristow
Nigel J. A. Bristow

P.S. Please tell us your success stories. We would love to learn from your experiences and celebrate your success. You can send these, along with your own personal folktales, to mj@stepchangelearning.com

---

"They know enough who know how to learn."

—Henry Adams

APPENDIX

CAREER ASSESSMENT

Read each pair of mindsets, and then indicate:
- Mindsets that you have bought into—and need to eliminate from your thinking in the future. (Indicate with an X)
- Mindsets that you need to cultivate more fully in the future. (Indicate with a √)

Low-Impact Mindsets	High-Impact Mindsets
❏ Receiving incentives and extrinsic rewards will make me feel better about myself.	❏ Making a difference and doing what I do best will make me feel better about myself.
❏ Incentives and extrinsic rewards are my top considerations when making career decisions.	❏ Fit and fulfillment are my top considerations when making career decisions.
❏ I make career choices based on what pays the best, and I'll worry about fit and fulfillment later.	❏ I make career choices based on fulfillment and fit, and later on I'll figure out how to make it pay.
❏ My job security depends on the success and stability of my company.	❏ My job security depends on my being employable and having realistic options.
❏ To persuade people to my way of thinking, I use persuasive logic and do most of the talking.	❏ To persuade people to my way of thinking, I spend most of my time asking questions and listening.
❏ My job security depends on what I have done in the past.	❏ My job security depends on what I am capable of in the future.
❏ My freedom to take stands and do what's right is tied to my formal power.	❏ My freedom to take stands and do what's right is tied to the number of genuine options I have and the strength of my safety net.

❏ Avoiding risks is a good career strategy.

❏ Not taking any risks is the riskiest career strategy around.

❏ Financial peace of mind is determined by how much money I make.

❏ Financial peace of mind is determined by what I do with what I make.

❏ I live from paycheck to paycheck. I use credit cards and other debt to make ends meet.

❏ I live well within my means and have the equivalent of three months' salary in savings.

❏ My influence in the organization is tied to my formal power.

❏ My influence in the organization is tied to the amount of value I add — my ability to serve the common good.

❏ Politics is a barrier to organization success.

❏ Politics is critical to the health and success of organizations.

❏ Careers are paths of ever- increasing status, formal power and pay.

❏ Careers are paths of ever-increasing ability and contribution.

❏ Someone higher in the organization is looking out for my career.

❏ If I don't look out for my own career, it's unlikely that anyone else will.

❏ My interests would be best served if someone at a higher level were to take responsibility for my career.

❏ When it comes to determining what is best for my career, I am the most qualified person. Only I can decide what will best serve my interests.

❑ I develop myself by identifying my weaknesses and fixing them.

❑ I develop myself by building on my strengths and managing my weaknesses.

❑ Incentives and rewards lead me to want to add more value at work. Contributions follow rewards.

❑ Adding more value at work leads the organization to reward me more generously. Rewards follow contributions.

❑ My job description represents what I'm expected to do at work.

❑ My job description represents a baseline expectation. I'm expected to add as much value as I can, and that often requires me to go beyond my job description.

❑ I'm paid to do what's in my job description, so the company must pay me more if they want me to do more.

❑ Even if I'm not paid more when I go beyond what's in my job description, I still win by learning things that make me more employable.

❑ My supervisor determines what I do at work.

❑ My supervisor and I jointly determine what I do at work.

❑ Change is a threat to my career success.

❑ Change is a source of career opportunities.

❑ Conflict is bad and should be avoided.

❑ Conflict is a catalyst for learning and should be managed.

❑ I spend time and partner with people who share my view of the world. It's more comfortable and less likely to trigger conflict.

❑ I spend time and partner with people who don't see the world the same way I do. It's less comfortable, but it helps me learn and accomplish a lot more.

❑ It is best to build teams with people who have similar strengths and perspectives.

❑ It is best to build teams with people who have diverse strengths and perspectives.

❑ People from a specific group or class will usually share the values and traits of that group.

❑ All people are unique, regardless of the groups they may be identified with. Rather than making assumptions about their values and traits, I try to get to know them as individuals.

❑ I am considerate and respectful towards the people I depend on or might need to depend on in the future.

❑ I am considerate and respectful towards everyone— even those who can be of no possible service to me.

❑ I can be successful without any help from others.

❑ Accomplishing great things at work is usually a team effort.

GETTING CONNECTED

Visit Our Website

To learn more about how Step Change Learning and the authors can help you or your company achieve world-class performance, go to: www.stepchangelearning.com

Other titles available from Step Change Learning:

The Beyond Job Satisfaction Fieldbook: Tools and Templates for Maximizing Your Engagement and Vitality at Work

Where's the Gift? Using Feedback to Work Smarter, Learn Faster and Avoid Disaster

To contact Step Change Learning:

Call us at 801-753-8882 or
email: info@stepchangelearning.com

To contact the authors:
mj@stepchangelearning.com
nigeljab@gmail.com

LEARNING MORE

Our Goals at Step Change Learning are:
1. To help organizations achieve world-class performance by fully engaging the talents and energies of their people,
2. To utilize the latest research in cognitive neuroscience and psychology to maximize employee development, performance, and leadership, and
3. To help individuals learn faster, work smarter, and achieve more.

Workshops and Coaching
- Building Customer Loyalty: Serving Both Customer and Company
- Compelling Presentations: Engaging Hearts and Minds
- Engage Yourself: Expanding Your Impact and Satisfaction at Work
- Essential Conversations: Connecting with Colleagues on the Most Vital Issues
- Step Change Mentoring: Powerful Partnerships, Remarkable Results
- The Step Change Leader: Driving Engagement and Results

Consulting and Speaking Engagements

Michael-John, as well as other Step Change Learning speakers and consultants, are available to speak and consult in the areas of:

- Leadership
- Talent Development and Retention
- Career Management
- Total Employee Engagement
- Receiving and Giving Feedback
- Coaching Skills
- Performance Management
- Influence without Authority
- Mentoring Skills

REFERENCES AND ADDITIONAL READING

For the especially studious reader, below are citations addressing all research discussed in this book, as well as additional books and articles that can provide additional insight. Enjoy! Or don't. The choice is yours.

Introduction
http://www.gallup.com/poll/181289/majority-employees-not-engaged-despite-gains-2014.aspx

Why Rhino Scatters His S#!T
Bristow, Nigel. The New Leadership Imperative. Orem, UT: Targeted Learning, 2000.

Burson, K.; Larrick, R.; Klayman, J. (2006). "Skilled or unskilled, but still unaware of it: how perceptions of difficulty drive miscalibration in relative comparisons." Journal of Personality and Social Psychology 90 (1): 5.

Cohen, A.R. and Bradford, D.L. Influence Without Authority. New York: John Wiley & Sons, 1990.

Kruger, Justin and Dunning, David (1999). "Unskilled and Unaware of It: How Difficulties in Recognizing One's Own Incompetence Lead to Inflated Self-Assessments." Journal of Personality and Social Psychology 77 (6): 1121–34.

Lee, Blaine. The Power Principle: Influence With Honor. New York: Simon and Schuster, 1998.

McRaney, David. You Are Not So Smart. New York: Penguin Group, 2011.

McRaney, David. You Are Now Less Dumb. New York: Penguin Group, 2013.

Nyhan, Brendan and Jason Reifler. "When Corrections Fail: The persistence of political misperceptions." Political Behavior, (2010): 32, 303-330.

Patterson, K.; Grenny, J.; McMillan, R.; A. Switzler. Crucial Conversations: Tools for Talking When Stakes are High. New York: McGraw Hill, 2002.

Pinchot, Gifford. Intrapreneuring: Why You Don't Have to Leave the Corporation to Become an Entrepreneur. New York: Harper and Row, 1985.

Segerstrom, S.C. "Optimism and resources: Effects on each other and on health over 10 years." Journal of research in personality 41, 4 (2007): 772-786.

Taylor, S. and Brown, J. (1994). "Positive Illusions and Well-Being Revisited Separating Fact From Fiction". American Psychological Association 116 (1): 21-27.

The Wisdom of Mongoose
Asch, S.E. (1951). "Effects of group pressure on the modification and distortion of judgments." In H. Guetzkow (Ed.), Groups, leadership and men (pp. 177–190). Pittsburgh, PA: Carnegie Press.

Asch, S.E. (1955). "Opinions and social pressure." Scientific American, 193, 35–35.

Bridges, William. Job Shift: How to Prosper in a Workplace without Jobs. Reading, MA: Addison Wesley, 1994.

Gould, S.B.; Weiner, K.J.; Levin, B.R. Free Agents. San Francisco: Jossey-Bass, 1997.

Hakim, Cliff. We Are All Self-Employed. San Francisco: Berrett-Koehler, 1994.

Klucharev, V.; Hytonen, K.; Rijpkema, M.; Smidts, A. Cell Press. "Brain Mechanisms Of Social Conformity." ScienceDaily. ScienceDaily, 16 January 2009.

Leonard, Thomas J. The Portable Coach. New York: Scribner, 1998.

Milgram, Stanley (1963). "Behavioral Study of Obedience". Journal of Abnormal and Social Psychology 67 (4): 371–8.

Milgram, Stanley (1974). Obedience to Authority; An Experimental View. HarperCollins, 1975.

Stanley, Thomas J. and Danko, William D. The Millionaire Next Door: The Surprising Secrets of America's Wealthy. New York: Simon & Schuster Trade, 1998.

Chicken and Dove

Achor, Shawn. The Happiness Advantage: The Seven Principles of Positive Psychology That Fuel Success and Performance at Work. New York: Random House, 2010.

Aknin, Lara B.; Norton, Michael I.; Dunn, Elizabeth W. (2009). "From wealth to well-being? Money matters, but less than people think." The Journal of Positive Psychology, 4 (6):523-527.

Brickman, P.; Coates, D.; Janoff-Bulman, R. (1978). "Lottery winners and accident victims: is happiness relative?" Journal of Personality and Social Psychology 36 (8): 917-27.

Bronson, Po. What Should I Do with My Life? New York: Random House, 2002.

Canfield, Jack and Miller, Jacqueline. Heart at Work. New York: McGraw Hill, 1996.

Carter, Christine (2008). "Happiness is being socially connected." http://greatergood.berkeley.edu/raising_happiness/post/happiness_is_being_socially_connected

Coulson, J. C.; McKenna, J.; Field, M. (2008). "Exercising at work and self-reported work performance." International Journal of Workplace Health Management 1 (3): 176-197.

Dunn, Elizabeth W.; Aknin, Laura B.; Norton, Michael I. (2008). "Spending Money on Others Promotes Happiness." Science 319 (5870): 1687-1688.

The Economist. "The U-bend of life." December 16, 2010.

Fowler, James H. and Christakis, Nicholas A. (2008). "Dynamic spread of happiness in a large social network: longitudinal analysis over 20 years in the Framingham Heart Study." BMJ 2008;337:a2338.

Gilbert, Daniel. Stumbling Upon Happiness. New York: Random House, 2006.

Jawbone (2015). "What makes people happy? We have the data."
https://jawbone.com/blog/what-makes-people-happy/

Jenkinson, Caroline E.; Dickens, Andy P.; Jones, Kerry; Thompson-Coon, Jo; Taylor, Rod S.; Rogers, Morwenna; Bambra, Clare L.; Lang, Iain.; Richards, Suzanne H. "Is volunteering a public health intervention? A systematic review and meta-analysis of the health and survival of volunteers." BMC Public Health 13: 773.

Killingsworth, Matthew A. and Gilbert, Daniel T. (2006). "A Wandering Mind Is an Unhappy Mind." Science 330 (6006): 932.

Kuhn, Peter J; Kooreman, Peter; Soetevent, Adriaan; Kapteyn, Arie (2008). "The Own and Social Effects of an Unexpected Income Shock: Evidence from the Dutch Postcode Lottery." Department of Economics, UCSB. UC Santa Barbara: Department of Economics, UCSB.

Kumar, Amit; Killingsworth, Matthew A.; Gilovich, Thomas (2014). "Waiting for Merlot: Anticipatory Consumption of Experiential and Material Purchases." Psychological Science 25 (10): 1924-1931.

Leider, Richard J. The Power of Purpose. New York: Ballantine Books, 1985.

Lyubomirsky, Sonja; Sheldon, Kennon M.; Schkade, David (2005). "Pursuing Happiness: The Architecture of Sustainable Change." Review of General Psychology 9 (2): 111-131.

McMahon, Darrin M. (2009). "Happiness, the Hard Way." http://greatergood.berkeley.edu/article/item/happiness_the_hard_way

Moss, Jennifer (2015). "Happiness Isn't the Absence of Negative Feelings." Harvard Business Review August 20, 2015.

Sandholtz, K., B. Derr; Buckner K.; Carlson, D. Beyond Juggling: Rebalancing Your Busy Life. San Francisco: Berrett Koehler, 2002.

Seligman, Martin. Flourish: A Visionary Understanding of Happiness and Wellbeing. New York: Simon & Schuster, 2011.

Scott, B. A. and Barnes, C. M. (2011). "A multilevel field investigation of emotional labor, affect, work withdrawal, and gender." Academy of Management Journal 54 (1): 116-136.

Stanley, Thomas J. and Danko, William D. The Millionaire Next Door: The Surprising Secrets of America's Wealthy. New York: Simon & Schuster Trade, 1998.

Stone, Arthur A.; Schwartz, Joseph E.; Broderick, Joan E.; Deaton, Angus (2010). "A snapshot of the age distribution of psychological well-being in the United States." Proceedings of the National Academy of Sciences of the United States of America 107 (22): 9985-9990.

Weiss, Alexander (2008). "Happiness Is a Personal(ity) Thing: The Genetics of Personality and Well-Being in a Representative Sample." Psychological Science 19 (3): 205-210.

A School for the Animals

Abramson, L. Y.; Seligman, M. E.; Teasdale, J. D. (1978, February). "Learned helplessness in humans: Critique and reformulation." Journal of Abnormal Psychology 87(1), 49–74.

Azevedo, T. M.; Volchan, E.; Imbiriba, L. A.;
Rodrigues, E. C.; Oliveira, J. M.; Oliveira, L. F.;
Lutterbach, L. G.; & Vargas, C. D. (2005, May).
"A freezing-like posture to pictures of mutilation."
Psychophysiology 42(3), 255–260.

Barthelmess, S. (1988, March/April). "Coming to grips
with panic." Flight Safety Foundation: Cabin Crew
Safety 23(2), 1–4.

Bolles, Richard N. What Color is Your Parachute?
Berkeley: Ten Speed Press, 2001.

Bristow, Nigel. Career Drivers: Achieving Career
Vitality Through Greater Self Knowledge. Orem:
Targeted Learning, 2000.

Cathcart, Jim. The Acorn Principle. New York: St.
Martin's Press, 1998.

Kroeger, Otto and Thuesen, Janet M. Type Talk: The 16
Personality Types that Determine How We Live, Love,
and Work. New York: Tilden Press, 1988.

Leach, J. (2004, June). "Why people 'freeze' in
an emergency: Temporal and cognitive constraints
on survival responses." Aviation, Space, and
Environmental Medicine 75(6), 539–542.

Leach, J. (2005). "Cognitive paralysis in an emergency:
The role of the supervisory attentional system."

Aviation, Space, and Environmental Medicine 76(2), 134–136.

Magnusson, D. and Ohman, A. (1987). Psychopathology: An interactional perspective. New York: Academic Press.

Mikami, S. and Ikeda, K. (1985). Human response to disasters. International Journal of Mass Emergencies and Disasters, 107–132.

Myers, D. G. (2005). Social psychology. New York: McGraw-Hill.

Seligman, M. and Maier, S.F. (1967). "Failure to escape traumatic shock." Journal of Experimental Psychology 74: 1–9.

Reeves, R.H. Teacher Training 2 (4), May 1948.

Ripley, Amanda. The Unthinkable: Who Survives When Disaster Strikes—and Why. New York: Random House, 2008.

The Bear Who Dared
Bridges, William. Managing Transitions. Reading, MA: Addison-Wesley,1991.

Covey, Stephen R. The 7 Habits of Highly Effective People. New York: Simon and Schuster, 1989.

Davis, Stan and Meyer, Christopher. BLUR—the Speed of Change in the Connected Economy. Reading, MA: Perseus Books, 1998.

Hutchens, David. Outlearning the Wolves. Waltham, MA: Pegasus Communications, 1998.

Johnson, Spencer. Who Moved My Cheese? New York: Putnam, 1998.

McClure, S. M.; Li, J.; Tomlin, D.; Cypert, K. S.; Montague, L. M.; Montague, P. R. (2004, October 14). "Neural correlates of behavioral preference for culturally familiar drinks." Neuron 44 (2), 379–387.

Scott, Cynthia and Joffe, Dennis. Take This Work and Love It. Menlo Park, CA: Crisp Publications, 1997.

Why Zebras Drink with Baboons

Abikoff, Howard; Courtney, Mary; Pelham, William E.; Koplewicz, Harold S. "Teachers' Ratings of Disruptive Behaviors: The Influence of Halo Effects." Journal of Abnormal Child Psychology 21, no. 5 (1993): 519–33.

Alessandra, Tony and O'Connor, M.J. The Platinum Rule. New York: Warner Books, 1996.
Goleman, Daniel. Emotional Intelligence. New York: Bantam, 1995.

Brewer, Gayle. "Height, Relationship Satisfaction, Jealousy, and Mate Retention." Evolutionary Psychology 7, no. 3 (2009): 477–89.

Bristow, Michael-John; Bristow, Nigel J. A. Where's the Gift? Using Feedback to Work Smarter, Learn Faster and Avoid Disaster. LCI Press, 2015.

Clifford, Margaret M. and Walster, Elaine. "The Effects of Physical Attractiveness on Teacher Expectations." Sociology of Education 46, no. 2 (1973): 248–58.

Dion, Karen; Berscheid, Ellen; Walster, Elaine. "What Is Beautiful Is Good." Journal of Personality and Social Psychology 24, no. 3 (1972): 285–90.

Eagly, Alice H.; Ashmore, Richard D.; Makhijani, Mona G.; Longo, Laura C. "What Is Beautiful Is Good, But...: A Meta-analytic Review of Research on the Physical Attractiveness Stereotype." Psychological Bulletin 110, no. 1 (1991): 109–28.

Efran, M. "The Effect of Physical Appearance on the Judgment of Guilt, Interpersonal Attraction, and Severity of Recommended Punishment in a Simulated Jury Task." Journal of Research in Personality 8, no. 1 (1974): 45–54.

Foster, Glen and Ysseldyke, James. "Expectancy and Halo Effects as a Result of Artificially Induced Teacher Bias." Contemporary Educational Psychology 1, no. 1 (1976): 37–45.

Goldin, Claudia and Rouse, Cecilia. "Orchestrating Impartiality: The Impact Of 'Blind' Auditions On

Female Musicians," American Economic Review, 2000, v90(4 Sep), 715-741.

Judge, Timothy A. and Cable, Daniel M. "The Effect of Physical Height on Workplace Success and Income: Preliminary Test of a Theoretical Model." Journal of Applied Psychology 89, no. 3 (2004): 428–41.

Kahneman, Daniel. Thinking, Fast and Slow. New York: Farrar, Straus and Giroux, 2011.

Kaplan, Robert M. "Is Beauty Talent? Sex Interaction in the Attractiveness Halo Effect." Sex Roles 4, no. 2 (1978): 195–204.

Landy, David and Sigall, Harold. "Beauty Is Talent: Task Evaluation as a Function of the Performer's Physical Attractiveness." Journal of Personality and Social Psychology 29, no. 3 (1974): 299–304.

Levitt, Steven D., and Dubner, Stephen J. Freakonomics: A Rogue Economist Explores the Hidden Side of Everything. New York: William Morrow, 2005.

Moore, F. R.; Filippou, D.; Perrett, D.I. "Intelligence and Attractiveness in the Face: Beyond the Attractiveness Halo Effect." Journal of Evolutionary Psychology 9, no. 3 (2011): 205–17.

Nisbett, Richard E. and Wilson, Timothy D. "The Halo Effect: Evidence for Unconscious Alteration of Judgments." Journal of Personality and Social Psychology 35, no. 4 (1977): 250–56.

Patterson, K.; Grenny, J.; McMillan, R.; Switzler, A. Crucial Conversations: Tools for Talking When Stakes are High. New York: Mcgraw Hill, 2002.

Rincon, Paul. "Newborns Prefer Beautiful Faces." BBC News, June 9, 2004.

Sigall, Harold and Ostrove, Nancy. "Beautiful but Dangerous: Effects of Offender Attractiveness and Nature of the Crime on Juridic Judgment." Journal of Personality and Social Psychology 31, no. 3 (1975): 410–14.

Slater, Alan. "Visual Perception in the Newborn Infant: Issues and Debates." Intellectica 1, no. 34 (2002): 57–76.

Thorndike, E. L. "A Constant Error in Psychological Ratings." Journal of Applied Psychology 4, no. 1 (1920): 25–29.

Williams, Mark A. and Clifton, David O. The 10 Lenses: Your Guide to Living in a Multicultural World. Washington DC: Capital Books, 2001.

Where on Earth is Timbuktu?

Andersen, Steffen; Ertaç, Seda; Gneezy, Uri; Hoffman, Moshe; List, John A. (2011). "Stakes Matter in Ultimatum Games." American Economic Review 101 (7): 3427–3439.

Bearden, Joseph Neil. Ultimatum Bargaining Experiments: The State of the Art (November 2001). Available at SSRN: http://ssrn.com/abstract=626183

Bellman, Geoffrey M. Getting Things Done When You Are Not in Charge. San Francisco: Berrett-Koehler, 1992.

Mackay, Harvey. Dig Your Well Before You're Thirsty. New York: Currency Doubleday, 1997.

Mueller, Robert K. Corporate Networking. New York: The Free Press, 1986.

Sanfey, Alan; Rilling, Aronson; Nystrom, Cohen (13 June 2003). "The Neural Basis of Economic Decision-Making in the Ultimatum Game." Science 300 (5626): 1755–1758.

Regan, Dennis T. (1971-11-01). "Effects of a favor and liking on compliance." Journal of Experimental Social Psychology 7 (6): 627–639.